HARDLY
IN THE KITCHEN

HARDLY
IN THE KITCHEN

Real meals in 20 minutes – 100 recipes
for the busy food lover

Steven Wheeler and Matthew Drennan

LORENZ BOOKS
NEW YORK • LONDON • SYDNEY • BATH

First published in the UK in 1997 by Lorenz Books

This edition published in the USA by Lorenz Books
27 West 20th Street, New York, New York 10011

LORENZ BOOKS are available for bulk purchase for sales promotion and for
premium use. For details write or call the manager of special sales:
Lorenz Books, 27 West 20th Street, New York, New York, 10011; (800) 354 9657

Lorenz Books is an imprint of
Anness Publishing Limited

ISBN 1 85967 424 0

Publisher: Joanna Lorenz
Senior Cookery Editor: Linda Fraser
In-house Editor: Anne Hildyard
Designer: Siân Keogh
Photographers: Edward Allwright, James Duncan, Michelle Garrett,
Amanda Heywood and Don Last
Additional Recipes: Maxine Clark, Christine France, Shirley Gill,
Carole Handslip, Sue Maggs, Annie Nichols, Jenny Stacey and Liz Trigg
Sylists: Madeleine Brehaut, Hilary Guy and Fiona Tillett

Printed and bound in Hong Kong

1 3 5 7 9 10 8 6 4 2

The material in this book previously appeared as individual titles in the *Step-by-Step* series.

CONTENTS

INTRODUCTION

With just 20 minutes to spare, it is possible to serve good food that hasn't come straight out of the freezer. *Hardly in the Kitchen* shows how easy it can be to produce a delicious lunch or supper in less time than it takes to reheat a TV dinner.

Although for many people fast food is necessary to keep up with their hectic lifestyles, fast food does not have to mean poor quality food. By mixing fresh produce with canned, dried or frozen food in tasty and innovative ways, you'll be amazed at the dishes you can produce in no time at all. The recipes in this book, such as Avocado, Tomato and Mozzarella Pasta Salad with Pine Nuts, Oriental Vegetable Noodles, and Glazed Lamb, all emphasize clever ingredient combinations that maximize flavor, color and texture and at the same time minimize the effort needed in preparation.

A well-stocked pantry and freezer are essential when speed is of the essence, as are using fast cooking techniques and having a well organized kitchen. The introduction provides essential information on ways to plan ahead, on what constitutes basic pantry ingredients and tips for sensible storage of food and equipment.

So even on the most hectic of days, with good ingredients that are fresh, colorful and appealing and with the help of this inspiring book, you'll be able to turn a speedy meal into a spread fit for a gourmet.

Planning ahead

Getting organized enough to serve a tasty, satisfying meal day after day can become difficult. For many, thinking of something to eat is the first problem, and cooking after a hard day at work can often seem like a chore. To make it as simple and effortless as possible, it's worth doing a little advance planning.

Start off with a shopping list that includes pantry staples and fresh produce. Good raw ingredients are essential and

Right: A colorful selection of fresh produce, including root vegetables, green vegetables and salad ingredients.

Below: Simple ingredients such as pasta, vegetables and cheese enlivened with fresh herbs make a quick and simple lunch or supper dish.

need less preparation and less seasoning. Avoid foods that sacrifice flavor for convenience. Fresh herbs or herb butter (prepared beforehand) add interest to simple dishes. Look

for ready-washed vegetables to save time at home. Buy fish fillets that are already boned and skinned, and meat that is prepared for cooking. To enliven pasta and rice dishes,

keep in a stock of pesto and other flavored sauces.

Storage of foods

When storing foods, separate sweet and savory ingredients, except those that are used for both such as flour, eggs and sugar. Ingredients that are used often, including onions, garlic, olive oil and fruit make an attractive display in the kitchen if there is space.

All ingredients should be used up and replaced regularly. Spices should be bought in small quantities as they lose flavor after several months and nuts become rancid if kept too long. Remember to check regularly and discard any foods that have gone past their sell-by dates. With a well-stocked pantry of basic foods in good condition, producing a tasty meal in 20 minutes need not seem too daunting.

Equipment

A few good saucepans in various sizes and with tight-fitting lids are a must. Heavy-based and non-stick pans are best. A large non-stick frying pan is invaluable to the quick cook. The food cooks faster when spread over a wide surface area. A wok is an essential tool for stir-frying,

Above: A wok is perfect for quick-cooking stir-fries and can also double as a steamer. Choose a heavy, non-stick wok for ease of cooking and save time washing up too.

Preparation
When chopping vegetables, cut them to the same size for speedy cooking. Start vegetables that take longer to cook first so that all the vegetables are ready at the same time.

Freeze extra grated cheese or breadcrumbs, ideal for later use.

Freeze stock in ice cube trays and use as required.

Stock the freezer with bread and frozen vegetables such as peas and broccoli, which do not require long cooking.

Above: A bowl of strawberries, crème fraîche and a ready-made flan case are all you need for an impromptu treat.

Below: A delicious selection of fresh fruit is perfect for a quick snack.

cooking food quickly and evenly in the minimum of oil, with no loss of nutrients. For efficiency, sharp knives save time and effort and are safer than blunt ones.

Use a food processor to take the hard work out of grating, blending, shredding and mixing.

Lastly, for speed and efficiency, keep your equipment close by, especially those labor-saving gadgets that are most frequently used.

Top: A good *batterie de cuisine* makes for efficiency in a kitchen where fast cooking is a priority.

Left: A heavy, non-stick frying pan allows food to spread over a large area and cook quickly and evenly.

Kitchen Cupboard Staples

The following ingredients are shown left to right from the top shelf.

Polenta
Italian cornmeal. Serve with Gorgonzola cheese and salad.

Flour
All-purpose and self-rising flour are used for making white sauces and pancakes.

Lentils
Red lentils soften quickly for simple soups and sauces.

Couscous
Cracked wheat for tabbouleh-style salads.

Sesame seeds
Nutty and rich when toasted. Sprinkle over an omelette.

Spices
Cumin, coriander, fennel seed, cardamom and peppercorns are best when freshly ground.

Pasta
Use best quality fine vermicelli for soups, and spaghetti and other pasta shapes with sauces.

Wild mushrooms
Deeply flavored dried porcini and morels revive in hot water.

Fresh herbs
Parsley, thyme, garlic and rosemary add instant flavor.

Long-grain and risotto rice
These take a little longer to cook but are full of flavor.

Almonds
These provide a rich flavor in sauces and salsas.

Buckwheat
Robustly flavored grain. Cook with couscous.

Garlic in oil
Garlic cloves keep their flavor in olive oil.

Tarragon in vinegar
Keep fresh tarragon in wine vinegar for year-round flavor.

Pine nuts
The intensely rich fruit of the pine cone. A great asset to vegetarian dishes.

Stock cubes
Good quality stock cubes are indispensable. Buy the additive-free type if you can.

Cornstarch
This is used for thickening sauces and gravies.

Capers
The fairly sharp taste of capers makes an ideal accompaniment to meat dishes.

Mustard
A piquant addition to meats and savory sauces.

Green peppercorns
Soft berries with an assertive heat. Delicious with pork.

Pesto sauce
Made from basil, garlic, pine nuts, cheese and olive oil. Use for speedy pasta dishes.

Pasta sauce
Make your own from a can of tomatoes. Serve with an Italian hard cheese.

Canned vegetables
Young peas and beans in brine are easy to serve with grilled meat and fish.

Citrus fruits
Bright oranges, lemons and limes offer fresh fruit flavors to savory cooking.

Onions
Onions, like garlic and ginger root, add delicious flavor to a variety of dishes.

Wine
Sober judgment allows a measure of wine, as and when it pleases the cook!

Oils
Keep olive oil for flavor, and a variety such as groundnut for neutral taste.

Vinegar
Use a good white wine vinegar. Balsamic vinegar should be used only sparingly.

Olives and pickled peppers
Good olives and pickled peppers will provide a taste of the sun in the winter.

Eggs
Fast-food convenience in a shell. Properly fed hens lay the best and tastiest eggs.

Dessert Kitchen Cupboard Staples

The following ingredients are shown left to right from the center shelf.

Flour
Plain and self-rising flour can be used for fast sponges, tarts and easy pancakes.

Superfine sugar
This is a free-flow, fast-mix, easy-blend sugar suited to all good cakes and baked goods.

Confectioners' sugar
This is powder-fine for easy icing and dusting. Sift before using to remove any lumps.

Meringues
Store-bought meringues kept in an airtight jar can be used for impromptu desserts.

Chocolate sauce
Make your own.
Delicious with ice cream, sprinkled with toasted nuts.

Cocoa powder
Use sugarless cocoa powder in drinks and desserts for a rich chocolate taste.

Chocolate
Buy the best quality chocolate you can afford and store it at room temperature, never in the refrigerator.

Cornstarch
Use this combined half-and-half with flour for fine textured cakes and sponges.

Citrus fruits
Oranges, lemons and limes offer zestful flavor. Heavy fruits offer the juiciest squeeze.

Cherries
Enjoy these fresh in season, as they have a poor flavor when cooked. Choose sour, or buy canned for cooking.

Melon
Fill your kitchen with the scent of a ripe melon. Serve cold with red berry fruit when in season.

Bananas
Bananas are deliciously sweet when speckled brown.

Pineapple
Pineapples are ripe when the skin smells sweet.

Strawberries
Traditionally served with sugar and cream, but also ideal for use in hot and cold desserts, cakes and tarts.

Pears
Partner pears with Parmesan, Pecorino, Gorgonzola or Roquefort cheeses.

Apples
Red, green and russet skins conceal a host of flavor. All these apples make a juicy and crisp addition to quick desserts.

Peaches
Remove the skins from sun-ripened peaches by plunging in boiling water.

Passionfruit
The sour, scented juice of this fruit is delicious when combined with strawberries and raspberries.

Grapes
There are innumerable varieties of grapes available, and they can be red, green or seedless. Muscat grapes offer the best flavor and sweetness.

Finger wafers
These and other ice cream accessories are a must for spur-of-the-moment desserts.

Brown sugar
Less refined than white, brown sugars are rich in molasses. Dark sugars are stronger in taste.

Flaked almonds
Uninteresting raw, a temptation when toasted. Scatter over ice cream, chocolate and summer fruit for the finishing touch.

Ground almonds
Essential for moist cakes and sponges; substitute half flour with ground almonds in any baking recipe.

Preserved fruit
Use canned or bottled apricots and raspberries for easy convenience in desserts.

Eggs
Store and use eggs at room temperature.

Crab and Egg Noodle Broth

This delicious broth is an ideal solution when you are hungry and time is short, and you need something fast, nutritious and filling.

COOK'S TIP
Fresh or frozen crab meat has the best flavor. Avoid canned crab, as this tastes rather bland.

Serves 4

INGREDIENTS
3 oz fine egg noodles
2 tbsp unsalted butter
1 small bunch scallions, chopped
1 celery stick, sliced
1 medium carrot, peeled and cut
    into sticks
5 cups chicken stock
4 tbsp dry sherry
4 oz white crab meat, fresh
    or frozen
pinch of celery salt
pinch of cayenne pepper
2 tsp lemon juice
1 small bunch cilantro or flat-leaf
    parsley, to garnish

1 Bring a large saucepan of salted water to a boil. Toss in the egg noodles and cook according to the instructions on the package. Cool under cold running water and leave immersed in water until required.

2 Heat the butter in another large pan, add the scallions, celery and carrot, cover and soften the vegetables over a gentle heat for 3–4 minutes.

3 Add the chicken stock and sherry, bring to a boil and simmer for a further 5 minutes.

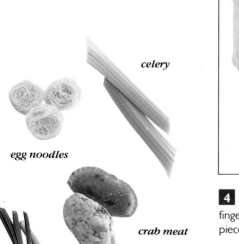

celery

egg noodles

crab meat

scallions

cilantro

4 Flake the crab meat between your fingers onto a plate and remove any stray pieces of shell.

5 Drain the noodles and add to the broth together with the crab meat. Season to taste with celery salt and cayenne pepper, and sharpen with the lemon juice. Return to a simmer.

6 Ladle the broth into shallow soup plates, scatter with roughly chopped cilantro or parsley and serve.

Broccoli and Almond Soup

The creaminess of the toasted almonds combines perfectly with the slight bitterness of the taste of broccoli.

Serves 4–6

INGREDIENTS
⅔ cup ground almonds
1 ½ lb broccoli
3¾ cups fresh vegetable stock or
     water
1 ¼ cups skim or low-fat milk
salt and freshly ground black pepper

ground almonds

skim milk

broccoli

1 Preheat the oven to 350°F. Spread the ground almonds evenly on a cookie sheet and toast in the oven for about 10 minutes, or until just golden. Reserve ¼ of the almonds and set aside for the garnish.

2 Cut the broccoli into small florets and steam for 6–7 minutes or until tender.

3 Place the remaining toasted almonds, broccoli, stock or water and milk in a blender and blend until smooth. Season to taste.

4 Reheat the soup and serve sprinkled with the reserved toasted almonds.

Chicken Vermicelli Soup with Egg Shreds

This soup is very quick and easy – you can add all sorts of extra ingredients to vary the taste, using up lurking leftovers such as scallions, mushrooms, a few shrimp, chopped salami and so on.

Serves 4–6

INGREDIENTS
3 large eggs
2 tbsp chopped fresh cilantro or
    parsley
6¼ cups good chicken stock or
    canned consommé
1 cup dried vermicelli or angel hair
    pasta
¼ lb cooked chicken breast, sliced
salt and pepper

vermicelli

chicken breast

eggs

cilantro

THAI CHICKEN SOUP

To make a Thai variation, use Chinese rice noodles instead of pasta. Stir ½ tsp dried lemon grass, 2 small whole fresh chilies and 4 tbsp coconut milk into the stock. Add 4 sliced scallions and plenty of chopped fresh cilantro.

1 First make the egg shreds. Whisk the eggs together in a small bowl and stir in the cilantro or parsley.

2 Heat a small nonstick skillet and pour in 2–3 tbsp egg, swirling to cover the base evenly. Cook until set. Repeat until all the mixture is used up.

3 Roll each pancake up and slice thinly into shreds. Set aside.

4 Bring the stock to a boil and add the pasta, breaking it up into short lengths. Cook for 3–5 minutes until the pasta is almost tender, then add the chicken, salt, and pepper. Heat through for 2–3 minutes, then stir in the egg shreds. Serve immediately.

French Onion Soup

In the time it takes to soften a few onions and brown some cheese on toast, this delicious soup appears on the table steaming hot and ready to eat. It makes a substantial starter or lunch dish.

Serves 4

INGREDIENTS
2 tbsp vegetable oil
3 medium onions, sliced
3¾ cups beef stock
4 slices French bread
butter, for spreading
1 cup grated Gruyère, Beaufort or
 Emmenthal cheese

onions

cheese

French bread

1 Heat the vegetable oil in a large frying pan and brown the onions over a steady heat, taking care they do not burn.

2 Transfer the browned onions to a large saucepan, cover with beef stock and simmer for 10 minutes.

3 Preheat the broiler to a moderate temperature and toast the French bread on both sides. Spread one side with butter and top with grated cheese. Ladle the soup into four flameproof dishes, float the cheesy crusts on top and grill until crispy and brown.

COOK'S TIP
The flavor and richness of French onion soup will improve if the soup is kept chilled in the refrigerator for three to four days.

Broiled New Zealand Mussels with Cumin

Large New Zealand mussels have a more distinctive flavor than the more common small black variety. If you can't find these the black mussels are also delicious prepared this way.

Serves 4

INGREDIENTS
3 tbsp fresh parsley
3 tbsp fresh cilantro
1 garlic clove, crushed
pinch of ground cumin
2 tbsp unsalted butter,
  softened
3 tbsp brown bread crumbs
freshly ground black pepper
12 New Zealand mussels or
  24 small mussels on the half-shell
chopped fresh parsley, to garnish

parsley

butter

garlic

bread

coriander

mussels

1 Chop the herbs finely.

2 Beat the garlic, herbs, cumin and butter together with a wooden spoon.

3 Stir in the bread crumbs and freshly ground black pepper.

4 Spoon a little of the mixture onto each mussel and broil for 2 minutes. Serve with chopped fresh parsley.

Deep-fried Florets with Tangy Thyme Mayonnaise

Cauliflower and broccoli make a sensational snack when coated in a beer batter and deep-fried. Serve with a tangy mayonnaise.

Serves 2–3

INGREDIENTS
6 oz cauliflower
6 oz broccoli
2 eggs, separated
2 tbsp olive oil
1 cup beer
1¼ cups all-purpose flour
pinch of salt
2 tbsp shredded fresh basil
vegetable oil for deep-frying
⅔ cup good quality mayonnaise
2 tsp chopped fresh thyme
2 tsp grated lemon rind
2 tsp lemon juice
sea salt, for sprinkling

eggs   *basil*   *all-purpose flour*

mayonnaise   *broccoli*

cauliflower   *beer*

thyme   *lemon*

1 Break the cauliflower and broccoli into small florets, cutting large florets into smaller pieces. Set aside.

2 Beat the egg yolks, olive oil, beer, flour and salt in a bowl. Strain the batter, if necessary, to remove any lumps.

3 Whisk the egg whites until stiff. Fold into the batter with the basil.

4 Heat the oil for deep-frying to 350°F or until a cube of bread, when added to the oil, browns in about 30–45 seconds. Dip the florets in the batter, and deep-fry in batches for 2–3 minutes until the coating is golden and crisp. Drain on paper towels.

5 Mix the mayonnaise, thyme, lemon rind and juice in a small bowl.

6 Sprinkle the florets with sea salt and then serve with the thyme mayonnaise.

Crispy "Seaweed" with Flaked Almonds

This popular appetizer in Chinese restaurants is in fact usually made not with seaweed but spring greens such as collard or chard! It is easy to make at home.

Serves 4-6

INGREDIENTS
1 lb spring greens
peanut oil, for deep-frying
¼ tsp sea salt flakes
1 tsp caster sugar
½ cup flaked almonds, toasted

spring greens

almonds

peanut oil

sea salt

sugar

COOK'S TIP
It is important to dry the spring greens thoroughly before deep-frying them, otherwise it will be difficult to achieve the desired crispness without destroying their vivid color.

1 Wash the spring greens under cold running water and then pat well with paper towels to dry thoroughly. Remove and discard the thick white stalks from the greens.

2 Lay several leaves on top of one another, roll up tightly and, using a sharp knife, slice as finely as possible into thread-like strips.

3 Half-fill a wok with oil and heat to 350°F. Deep-fry the greens in batches for about 1 minute until they darken and crisp. Remove each batch from the wok as soon as it is ready and drain on paper towels.

4 Transfer the "seaweed" to a serving dish, sprinkle with the salt and sugar, then mix well. Garnish with the toasted flaked almonds sprinkled over.

Hot Spicy Crab Claws

Crab claws are used to delicious effect in this quick appetizer based on an Indonesian dish called *Kepiting Pedas*.

Serves 4

INGREDIENTS
12 fresh or frozen and thawed
   cooked crab claws
4 shallots, coarsely chopped
2-4 fresh red chilies, seeded and
   coarsely chopped
3 garlic cloves, coarsely chopped
1 tsp grated fresh ginger
½ tsp ground coriander
3 tbsp peanut oil
4 tbsp water
2 tsp sweet soy sauce
   (kecap manis)
2-3 tsp lime juice
salt, to taste
fresh cilantro, to garnish

shallots

crab claws

sweet soy sauce

garlic

coriander

red chilies   *peanut oil*

lime

ginger

1 Crack the crab claws with the back of a heavy knife to make eating easier. Set aside. In a mortar, pound the chopped shallots with the pestle until pulpy. Add the chilies, garlic, ginger and ground coriander and pound until the mixture forms a coarse paste.

2 Heat the wok over medium heat. Add the oil and swirl it around. When it is hot, stir in the chili paste. Stir-fry for about 30 seconds. Increase the heat to high. Add the crab claws and stir-fry for another 3–4 minutes.

3 Stir in the water, sweet soy sauce, lime juice and salt to taste. Continue to stir-fry for 1–2 minutes. Serve at once, garnished with fresh cilantro. The crab claws are eaten with the fingers, so provide finger bowls.

COOK'S TIP
If whole crab claws are unavailable, look out for frozen prepared crab claws. These are shelled with just the tip of the claw attached to the white meat. Stir-fry for about two minutes until heated through.

Butterfly Shrimp

Use raw shrimp if you can because the flavor will be better, but if you substitute cooked shrimp, cut down the stir-fry cooking time by one third.

Serves 4

INGREDIENTS
1 in piece ginger root
12 oz raw shrimp, thawed
 if frozen
½ cup raw peanuts, roughly
 chopped
3 tbsp vegetable oil
1 clove garlic, crushed
1 red chili, finely chopped
3 tbsp smooth peanut butter
1 tbsp fresh cilantro, chopped
fresh cilantro sprigs, to garnish

FOR THE DRESSING
⅔ cup natural low-fat yogurt
2 in piece cucumber, diced
salt and freshly ground black pepper

diced cucumber

peanuts

shrimp

coriander

chili

1 To make the dressing, mix together the yogurt, cucumber and seasoning in a bowl, then leave to chill while preparing and cooking the shrimp.

2 Peel the ginger, and chop it finely.

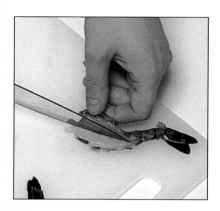

3 Prepare the shrimp by peeling off the shells, leaving the tails intact. Make a slit down the back of each shrimp and remove the black vein, then slit the shrimp completely down the back and open it out to make a "butterfly."

4 Heat the wok and dry-fry the peanuts, stirring constantly until golden brown. Leave to cool. Wipe out the wok with paper towels.

5 Heat the wok, add the oil and when hot add the ginger, garlic and chili. Stir-fry for 2–3 minutes until the garlic is softened but not brown.

6 Add the shrimp, then increase the heat and stir-fry for 1–2 minutes until the shrimp turn pink. Stir in the peanut butter and stir-fry for 2 minutes. Add the chopped cilantro, then scatter in the peanuts. Garnish with cilantro sprigs and serve with the cucumber dressing.

Smoked Salmon Crêpes with Pesto and Pine Nuts

These simple crêpes take no more than 10–15 minutes to prepare and are perfect for a special occasion. Smoked salmon is delicious with fresh basil and combines well with toasted pine nuts and a spoonful of crème fraîche or heavy cream.

Makes 12–16

INGREDIENTS
½ cup milk
1 cup self-rising flour
1 egg
2 tbsp pesto sauce
vegetable oil, for frying
scant 1 cup crème fraîche or heavy cream
3 oz smoked salmon
1 tbsp pine nuts, toasted
salt and freshly ground black pepper
12–16 fresh basil sprigs, to garnish

basil

pine nuts

crème fraîche

flour

pesto sauce

smoked salmon

1 Pour half of the milk into a mixing bowl. Add the flour, egg, pesto sauce and seasoning and mix to a smooth batter.

2 Add the remainder of the milk and stir until evenly blended.

3 Heat the vegetable oil in a large frying pan. Spoon the crêpe mixture into the heated oil in small heaps. Allow about 30 seconds for the crêpes to cook, then turn and cook briefly on the other side. Continue cooking the crêpes in batches until all the batter is used up.

4 Arrange the crêpes on a serving plate and top each one with a spoonful of crème fraîche or heavy cream.

5 Cut the salmon into 1 cm/½ in strips and place on top of each crêpe.

COOK'S TIP

If not serving immediately, cover the crêpes with a dish towel and keep warm in an oven preheated to 275°F.

6 Scatter each crêpe with pine nuts and garnish with a sprig of fresh basil.

Chicken Goujons

Serve as a first course for eight people or as a filling main course for four. Delicious served with new potatoes and salad.

Serves 8

INGREDIENTS
4 boned and skinned chicken breasts
3 cups fresh bread crumbs
1 tsp ground coriander
½ tsp ground paprika
½ tsp ground cumin
3 tbsp all-purpose flour
2 eggs, beaten
oil, for deep-frying
salt and freshly ground black pepper
lemon slices, to garnish
sprigs of fresh cilantro, to garnish

FOR THE DIP
1¼ cups plain yogurt
2 tbsp lemon juice
4 tbsp chopped fresh cilantro
4 tbsp chopped fresh parsley

bread crumbs

flour

eggs

lemon

yogurt

cilantro

parsley

chicken breast

1 Divide the chicken breasts into two natural fillets. Place them between two sheets of plastic wrap and, using a rolling pin, flatten each one to a thickness of about ¼ in.

2 Cut into 1 in strips diagonally across the fillets.

3 Mix the bread crumbs with the spices and seasoning. Toss the chicken fillet pieces (goujons) into the flour, keeping them separate.

4 Dip the fillets into the beaten egg and then coat in the bread crumb mixture.

5 Thoroughly mix all the ingredients for the dip together, and season to taste. Chill until required.

6 Heat the oil in a heavy-based pan. It is ready for deep-frying when a cube of bread tossed into the oil sizzles on the surface. Fry the goujons in batches until golden and crisp. Drain on paper towels and keep warm in the oven until all the chicken has been fried. Garnish with lemon slices and sprigs of fresh cilantro.

Filled Croissants

Croissants are very versatile and can be used with sweet or savory fillings.

Makes 2

INGREDIENTS
2 croissants
knob of butter
2 eggs
salt and pepper
1 tablespoon heavy cream
2 oz smoked salmon, chopped
1 sprig fresh dill, to garnish

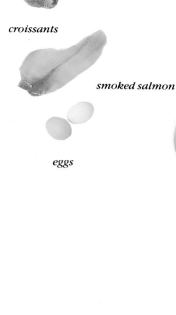

croissants

smoked salmon

eggs

1 Preheat the oven to 350°F. Slice the croissants in half horizontally and warm in the oven for 5–6 minutes.

2 Melt a knob of butter in a small pan. Beat the eggs in a bowl with seasoning to taste.

3 Add the eggs to the pan and cook for 2 minutes, stirring constantly.

4 Remove from the heat and stir in the cream and smoked salmon.

5 Spoon the smoked salmon mixture into the warmed croissants and garnish.

PEAR AND STILTON FILLING

Soften 4 oz Stilton cheese with a fork and mix in 1 peeled, cored, and chopped ripe pear and 1 tbsp chopped chives with a little black pepper. Spoon into a split croissant and bake in a preheated oven for 5 minutes.

Soufflé Omelet

This delectable soufflé omelet is light and delicate enough to melt in your mouth.

Serves 1

INGREDIENTS
2 eggs, separated
2 tbsp cold water
1 tbsp chopped fresh cilantro
salt and freshly ground black pepper
½ tbsp olive oil
2 tbsp mango chutney
¼ cup Jarlsberg or Swiss cheese,
  grated

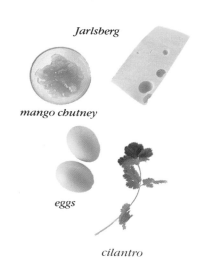

Jarlsberg

mango chutney

eggs

cilantro

COOK'S TIP

A light hand is essential to the success of this dish. Do not overmix the egg whites into the yolks or the mixture will be heavy.

1 Beat the egg yolks together with the cold water, cilantro and seasoning.

2 Whisk the egg whites until stiff but not dry and gently fold into the egg yolk mixture.

3 Heat the oil in a frying pan, pour in the egg mixture and reduce the heat. Do not stir. Cook until the omelet becomes puffy and golden brown on the underside (carefully lift one edge with a spatula to check).

4 Spoon on the chutney and sprinkle on the Jarlsberg. Fold over and slide onto a warm plate. Eat immediately. (If preferred, before adding the chutney and cheese, place the pan under a hot broiler to set the top.)

Fritters

A variation on beef patties, coated in batter and lightly fried, this tasty alternative need only be served with a light salad to provide a substantial snack.

Serves 4

INGREDIENTS
FOR THE PATTIES
8 oz/2 cups ground beef
1 onion, grated
2 tsp chopped fresh oregano
½ cup canned corn, drained
1 tsp mustard
2 cups fresh white bread crumbs
oil for deep-frying
salt and freshly ground black pepper

FOR THE BATTER
1 cup flour
¼ cup warm water
3 tbsp melted butter
¼ cup cold water
1 egg white

ground beef

onion

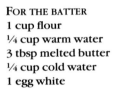
corn

bread crumbs

butter

oregano

mustard

1 For the patties, place the ground beef in a bowl and mash with a fork. Add the onion, oregano, corn, mustard and bread crumbs. Season well.

2 Form into eight round patties with lightly floured hands.

3 For the batter, sift the flour into a bowl and stir in the warm water and melted butter. Mix to a smooth batter with the cold water. Whisk the egg white until peaking and fold into the mixture.

4 Heat the oil for deep-frying to 325°F. Dip the patties into the batter to coat and fry two at a time in the oil. Drain on paper towels and serve with tomato pickle and green salad.

Tomato Omelet Envelopes

Delicious chive omelet, folded and filled with a tasty tomato mixture and lots of melting Camembert cheese.

Serves 2

INGREDIENTS
1 small onion
4 tomatoes
2 tbsp vegetable oil
4 eggs
2 tbsp chopped fresh chives
4 oz Camembert cheese, rind
  removed and diced
salt and freshly ground black pepper

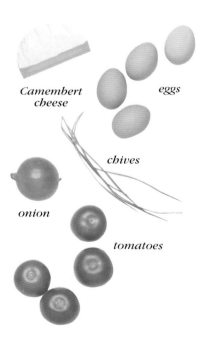

Camembert cheese

eggs

chives

onion

tomatoes

1 Cut the onion in half. Cut each half into thin wedges. Cut the tomatoes into wedges of similar size.

2 Heat 1 tbsp of the oil in a frying pan. Cook the onion for 2 minutes over a moderate heat. Then raise the heat, and add the tomato wedges. Cook for 2 minutes more. Then remove the pan from the heat.

3 Beat the eggs with the chives in a bowl. Add salt and pepper to taste. Heat the remaining oil in an omelet pan. Add half the egg mixture, and tilt the pan to spread thinly. Cook for 1 minute.

4 Flip the omelet over, and cook for 1 minute more. Remove from the pan, and keep hot. Make a second omelet with the remaining egg mixture.

5 Return the tomato mixture to a high heat. Add the cheese, and toss the mixture over the heat for 1 minute.

6 Divide the mixture between the omelets, and fold them over. Serve at once. Add crisp lettuce leaves and chunks of whole wheat bread, if desired.

COOK'S TIP
You may need to wipe the pan clean between the omelets, and reheat a little more oil.

Croque Monsieur

Probably the most popular snack food in France, this hot cheese and ham sandwich can be either pan-fried or broiled.

Makes 2

INGREDIENTS
4 slices white bread
2 tbsp softened butter
2 thin slices lean ham
2 oz Swiss cheese, thinly sliced
1 sprig flat-leaf parsley, to garnish

white bread

Swiss cheese

ham

COOK'S TIP

A flavored butter can be used to complement a sandwich filling – for example, horseradish butter with beef, mustard butter with ham, lemon and dill butter with fish. To make these just beat the chosen flavoring into the softened butter with some seasoning. Other useful flavorings for butter are: anchovy or curry paste, garlic, herbs, Tabasco, or chili. These butters can also be used in open-face sandwiches.

1 Spread the bread with butter.

2 Lay the ham on 2 of the buttered sides of bread.

3 Lay the Swiss cheese slices on top of the ham and sandwich with the buttered bread slices. Press firmly together and cut off the crusts.

4 Spread the top with butter, place on a rack, and cook for 2½ minutes under the broiler preheated to a low to moderate temperature.

5 Turn the sandwiches over, spread the remaining butter over the top, and return to the broiler for 2½ minutes more, until the bread is golden brown and the cheese is beginning to melt. Garnish with a sprig of flat-leaf parsley.

Sardines with Warm Herb Salsa

Plain grilling is the very best way to cook fresh sardines; served with this luscious herb salsa the only other essential item is fresh, crusty bread, to mop up the tasty juices.

Serves 4

12–16 fresh sardines
oil for brushing
juice of 1 lemon

FOR THE SALSA
1 tbsp butter
4 scallions, chopped
1 garlic clove, finely chopped
2 tbsp finely chopped fresh
  parsley
2 tbsp finely snipped fresh
  chives
2 tbsp finely chopped fresh
  basil
2 tbsp green olive paste
2 tsp balsamic vinegar
zest of 1 lemon
salt and freshly ground black
  pepper

sardines

butter

green olive paste

balsamic vinegar

lemon

scallions

parsley

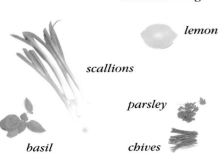

basil   *chives*

1 To clean the sardines, use small scissors to slit them along the belly and pull out the innards. Wipe the fish with paper towels and then arrange on a grill rack.

2 Melt the butter and gently sauté the scallions and garlic for about 2 minutes, shaking the pan occasionally, until softened but not browned.

3 Add the lemon rind and remaining ingredients and keep warm on the edge of the barbecue. Do not allow to boil.

4 Brush the sardines lightly with oil and sprinkle with lemon juice, salt and pepper. Cook for about 2 minutes on each side, over a moderate heat. Serve with the warm salsa and crusty bread.

Chili Beef Tacos

These easy-to-prepare sandwiches are now equally at home on both sides of the border. But don't limit yourself to the taco shell, soft flour tortillas are also authentically Mexican.

Makes 4

INGREDIENTS
1 tbsp oil
1 small onion, chopped
2 garlic cloves, chopped
6 oz ground beef
½ tbsp flour
7 oz can tomatoes
½ tbsp finely chopped Jalapeño
   peppers
salt
4 wheat or corn tortillas
3 tbsp sour cream
½ avocado, peeled, pitted and sliced
1 tomato, sliced
Tomato Salsa, to serve (optional)

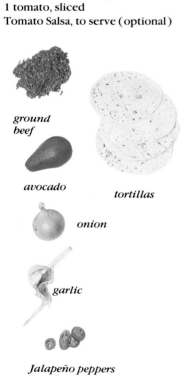

*ground
beef*

avocado

tortillas

onion

garlic

Jalapeño peppers

1 Heat the oil in a skillet, add the onion, and fry until softened. Add the garlic and beef and cook, stirring so that the meat is broken up as it sears.

2 Stir in the flour, then add the canned tomatoes, peppers, and salt to taste.

3 Heat the tortillas one at a time in a medium-hot lightly oiled pan.

4 Spread a spoonful of the meat mixture over each tortilla.

5 Top each tortilla with some sour cream and avocado and tomato slices. Roll up and eat immediately with Tomato Salsa if liked.

Tostadas with Refried Beans

A tostada is a crisp, fried tortilla used as a base on which to pile the topping of your choice – a variation on a sandwich and a very tasty snack popular on both sides of the border.

Makes 6

INGREDIENTS
2 tbsp oil
1 onion, chopped
2 garlic cloves, chopped
½ tsp chili powder
15 oz can borlotti or pinto beans, drained
⅔ cup chicken stock
1 tbsp tomato paste
2 tbsp chopped fresh cilantro
salt and pepper
6 corn tortillas
3 tbsp Tomato Salsa
2 tbsp sour cream
½ cup grated Cheddar cheese
fresh cilantro leaves, to garnish

beans

onion

garlic

tomato paste

tortillas

chili powder

Cheddar cheese

cilantro

1 Heat the oil in a pan and fry the onion until softened.

2 Add the garlic and chili powder and fry for 1 minute, stirring.

3 Mix in the beans and mash very roughly with a potato masher.

4 Add the stock, tomato paste, chopped cilantro, and seasoning to taste. Mix thoroughly and cook for a few minutes.

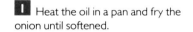

5 Fry the tortillas in hot oil for 1 minute, turning once, until crisp, then drain on paper towels.

TOMATO SALSA

Makes about 1¼ cups

1 small onion, chopped
1 garlic clove, crushed
2 fresh green chilies, seeded and
    finely chopped, or 1 tsp bottled
    chopped chilies
1 lb tomatoes, skinned and chopped
salt
2 tbsp chopped fresh cilantro

Stir all the ingredients together until
well mixed.

6 Put a spoonful of refried beans on
each tostada, spoon over some Tomato
Salsa, then some sour cream, sprinkle
with grated Cheddar cheese, and garnish
with cilantro.

Deep-fried Whitebait

A spicy coating on these fish gives this favourite dish a crunchy bite.

Serves 6

INGREDIENTS
1 cup flour
½ tsp curry powder
½ tsp ground ginger
½ tsp ground cayenne pepper
pinch of salt
2½ lb fresh or frozen whitebait, thawed
vegetable oil for deep-frying
lemon wedges, to garnish

cayenne pepper

ground ginger

curry powder

lemon

whitebait

1 Mix together all the dry ingredients in a large bowl.

2 Coat the fish in the flour.

3 Heat the oil in a large, heavy-based saucepan until it reaches a temperature of 375°F. Fry the whitebait in batches for 2–3 minutes until the fish is golden and crispy.

4 Drain well on absorbent paper towels. Serve hot garnished with lemon wedges.

Spiced Chicken Livers

Chicken livers can be bought frozen, but make sure that you defrost them thoroughly before using. Serve as a first course or light meal along with a mixed salad and garlic bread.

Serves 4

INGREDIENTS

12 oz chicken livers
1 cup all-purpose flour
½ tsp ground coriander
½ tsp ground cumin
½ tsp ground cardamom seeds
¼ tsp ground paprika
¼ tsp ground nutmeg
6 tbsp olive oil
salt and freshly ground black pepper
garlic bread, to serve

chicken livers

olive oil

flour

coriander

cardamom seeds

cumin

paprika

nutmeg

1 Dry the chicken livers on paper towels, removing any unwanted pieces. Cut the large livers in half and leave the smaller ones whole.

2 Mix the flour with all the spices and the seasoning.

3 Coat the first batch of livers with spiced flour, separating each piece. Heat the oil in a large frying pan and fry the livers in small batches. (This helps to keep the oil temperature high and prevents the flour from becoming soggy.)

4 Fry quickly, stirring frequently, until crispy. Keep warm and repeat with the remaining livers. Serve immediately with warm garlic bread.

Cucumber and Alfalfa Tortillas

Wheat tortillas are extremely simple to prepare at home. Served with a crisp, fresh salsa, they make a marvelous light lunch or supper dish.

COOK'S TIP
When peeling the avocado be sure to scrape off the bright green flesh from immediately under the skin as this gives the sauce its vivid green color.

Serves 4

INGREDIENTS
2 cups flour, sifted
pinch of salt
3 tbsp olive oil
½-⅔ cup warm water
lime wedges, to garnish

FOR THE SALSA
1 red onion, finely chopped
1 fresh red chili, seeded and finely chopped
2 tbsp chopped fresh dill or cilantro
½ cucumber, peeled and chopped
6 oz alfalfa sprouts

FOR THE SAUCE
1 large ripe avocado, peeled and pitted
juice of 1 lime
2 tbsp soft goat cheese
pinch of paprika

avocado

goat cheese

red chilli

cucumber

dill

alfalfa sprouts

1 Mix all the salsa ingredients together in a bowl and set aside.

2 To make the sauce, place the avocado, lime juice and goat cheese in a food processor or blender and blend until smooth. Place in a bowl and cover with plastic wrap. Dust with paprika just before serving.

3 To make the tortillas, place the flour and salt in a food processor, add the oil and blend. Gradually add the water (the amount will vary depending on the type of flour). Stop adding water when a stiff dough has formed. Turn out onto a floured board and knead until smooth. Cover with a damp cloth.

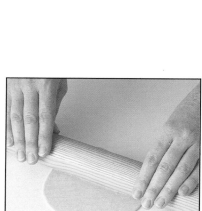

4 Divide the mixture into 8 pieces. Knead each piece for a couple of minutes and form into a ball. Flatten and roll out each ball to a 9 in circle.

5 Heat an ungreased cast-iron pan. Cook 1 tortilla at a time for about 30 seconds on each side. Place the cooked tortillas in a clean dish-towel and repeat until you have 8 tortillas.

6 To serve, spread each tortilla with a spoonful of avocado sauce, top with salsa and roll up. Garnish with lime wedges.

Stilton Burger

Slightly more up-market than the traditional burger, this tasty recipe contains a delicious surprise. The lightly melted Stilton cheese encased in a crunchy burger is absolutely delicious.

Serves 4

INGREDIENTS
1 lb/4 cups ground beef
1 onion, finely chopped
1 celery stalk, chopped
1 tsp dried mixed herbs
1 tsp prepared mustard
½ cup crumbled Stilton cheese
4 burger buns
salt and freshly ground black pepper

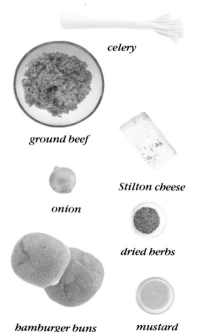

celery

ground beef

Stilton cheese

onion

dried herbs

hamburger buns

mustard

1 Place the ground beef in a bowl together with the onion and celery. Season well.

2 Stir in the herbs and mustard, bringing them together to form a firm mixture.

3 Divide the mixture into eight equal portions. Place four on a chopping board and flatten each one slightly.

4 Place the crumbled cheese in the center of each.

5 Flatten the remaining mixture and place on top. Mold the mixture together encasing the crumbled cheese and shape into four burgers.

6 Grill under a medium heat for 10 minutes, turning once or until cooked through. Split the hamburger buns and place a burger inside each. Serve with salad, ketchup, and mustard pickle.

Nachos

The addition of beef to this Mexican appetizer makes a hearty meal. Guacamole on the side makes the dish even more delicious.

Serves 4

INGREDIENTS
8 oz/2 cups ground beef
2 red chilies, chopped
3 scallions, chopped
6 oz nachos
1¼ cups sour cream
½ cup freshly grated medium-sharp
   Cheddar cheese
salt and freshly ground black pepper

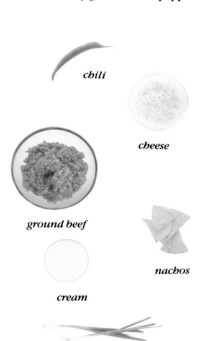

chili

cheese

ground beef

nachos

cream

scallions

1 Dry-fry the ground beef and chilies in a large pan for 10 minutes, stirring all the time.

2 Add the scallions, season and cook for a further 5 minutes.

3 Arrange the nachos in four individual flameproof dishes.

4 Spoon on the ground beef mixture, top with sour cream and grated cheese. Broil under a medium heat for 5 minutes.

Margherita

(Tomato, Basil and Mozzarella)
This classic pizza is simple to prepare. The sweet flavour of sun-ripened tomatoes works wonderfully with the basil and mozzarella.

Serves 2–3

INGREDIENTS
1 pizza base, about 10–12 in diameter
2 tbsp olive oil
1 quantity Tomato Sauce
5 oz mozzarella
2 ripe tomatoes, thinly sliced
6–8 fresh basil leaves
2 tbsp freshly grated Parmesan
black pepper

basil

mozzarella

Parmesan

olive oil

tomatoes

Tomato Sauce

1 Preheat the oven to 425°F. Brush the pizza base with 1 tbsp of the oil and then spread over the Tomato Sauce.

2 Cut the mozzarella into thin slices.

3 Arrange the sliced mozzarella and tomatoes on top of the pizza base.

4 Roughly tear the basil leaves, add and sprinkle with the Parmesan. Drizzle over the remaining oil and season with black pepper. Bake for 15–20 minutes until crisp and golden. Serve immediately.

Breaded Eggplant with Hot Vinaigrette

Crisp on the outside, beautifully tender within, these eggplant slices taste wonderful with a spicy dressing flavored with chili and capers.

COOK'S TIP
When serving a salad with a warm dressing, use robust leaves that will stand up to the heat.

Serves 2

INGREDIENTS
1 large eggplant
$^1/_2$ cup all-purpose flour
2 eggs, beaten
2 cups fresh white bread crumbs
vegetable oil for frying
1 head radicchio
salt and freshly ground black pepper

FOR THE DRESSING
2 tbsp olive oil
1 garlic clove, crushed
1 tbsp capers, drained
1 tbsp white wine vinegar
1 tbsp chili oil

eggplant

bread crumbs

eggs

all-purpose flour

radicchio

capers

white wine vinegar

garlic clove

1 Remove the ends from the eggplant. Cut it into $^1/_4$ in slices. Set aside.

2 Season the flour with a generous amount of salt and black pepper. Spread out in a shallow dish. Pour the beaten eggs into a second dish. Spread out the bread crumbs in a third.

3 Dip the eggplant slices in the flour, then in the beaten egg and finally in the bread crumbs, patting them on to make an even coating.

4 Pour vegetable oil into a large frying pan to a depth of about $^1/_4$ in. Heat the oil, then fry the eggplant slices for 3–4 minutes, turning once. Drain well on paper towels.

5 Heat the olive oil in a small pan. Add the garlic and the capers, and cook over gentle heat for 1 minute. Increase the heat, add the vinegar, and cook for 30 seconds. Stir in the chili oil, and remove the pan from the heat.

6 Arrange the radicchio leaves on two plates. Top with the hot eggplant slices. Drizzle over the vinaigrette, and serve.

Spiced Coconut Mushrooms

Here is a simple and delicious way to cook mushrooms. They may be served with almost any Asian meal as well as with grilled or roasted meats and poultry.

Serves 3–4

INGREDIENTS
2 tbsp peanut oil
2 garlic cloves, finely chopped
2 fresh red chilies, seeded and
  sliced into rings
3 shallots, finely chopped
225 g/8 oz crimini or button
  mushrooms, thickly sliced
⅔ cup coconut milk
2 tbsp fresh cilantro,
  finely chopped
salt and ground black pepper

red chilies

coconut milk

mushrooms

peanut oil

cilantro

garlic

VARIATION
Use chopped fresh chives instead of cilantro if you wish.

1 Heat a wok until hot, add the oil and swirl it around. Add the garlic and chilies, then stir-fry for a few seconds.

2 Add the shallots and stir-fry for 2–3 minutes, until softened. Add the mushrooms and stir-fry for 3 minutes.

3 Pour in the coconut milk and bring to a boil. Boil rapidly over high heat until the liquid is reduced by half and coats the mushrooms. Taste and adjust the seasoning, if necessary.

4 Sprinkle over the cilantro and toss gently to mix. Serve at once.

Stir-fried Chickpeas

Buy canned chickpeas and you will save all the time needed for soaking and then thoroughly cooking dried chickpeas. Served with a crisp green salad, this dish makes a filling vegetarian main course for two, or could be served in smaller quantities as a starter or side dish.

Serves 2–4 as an accompaniment

INGREDIENTS

2 tbsp sunflower seeds
1 × 14 oz can chickpeas, drained
    and rinsed
1 tsp chili powder
1 tsp paprika
2 tbsp vegetable oil
1 clove garlic, crushed
7 oz canned chopped tomatoes
8 oz fresh spinach, well washed and
    coarse stalks removed
salt and freshly ground black pepper
2 tsp chili oil

spinach

garlic

sunflower seeds

chickpeas

1 Heat the wok, and then add the sunflower seeds. Dry-fry until the seeds are golden and toasted.

2 Remove the sunflower seeds and set aside. Toss the chickpeas in chili powder and paprika. Remove and reserve.

3 Heat the wok, then add the oil. When the oil is hot, stir-fry the garlic for 30 seconds, add the chickpeas and stir-fry for 1 minute.

4 Stir in the tomatoes and stir-fry for 4 minutes. Toss in the spinach, season well and stir-fry for 1 minute. Drizzle chili oil and scatter sunflower seeds over the vegetables, then serve.

Asparagus Rolls with Herb Butter Sauce

For a taste sensation, try tender asparagus spears wrapped in crisp filo pastry. The buttery herb sauce makes the perfect accompaniment.

Serves 2

INGREDIENTS
4 sheets of filo pastry
¼ cup butter, melted
16 young asparagus spears, trimmed

FOR THE SAUCE
2 shallots, finely chopped
1 bay leaf
⅔ cup dry white wine
6 oz butter, softened
1 tbsp chopped fresh herbs
salt and freshly ground black pepper
chopped chives, to garnish

fresh herbs

chives

dry white wine

asparagus spears

filo pastry *butter*

bay leaf *shallots*

1 Preheat the oven to 400°F. Cut the filo sheets in half. Brush a half sheet with melted butter. Fold one corner of the sheet down to the bottom edge to give a wedge shape.

2 Lay 4 asparagus spears on top at the longest edge, and roll up toward the shortest edge. Using the remaining filo and asparagus spears, make three more rolls in the same way.

3 Lay the rolls on a greased baking sheet. Brush with the remaining melted butter. Bake in the oven for 8 minutes until golden.

4 Meanwhile, put the shallots, bay leaf and wine into a pan. Cover, and cook over a high heat until the wine is reduced to 3–4 tbsp.

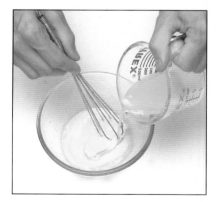

5 Strain the wine mixture into a bowl. Whisk in the butter, a little at a time, until the sauce is smooth and glossy.

6 Stir in the herbs, and add salt and pepper to taste. Return to the pan, and keep the sauce warm. Serve the rolls on individual plates with a salad garnish, if desired. Serve the sauce separately, sprinkled with a few chopped chives.

Chinese Greens with Oyster Sauce

Here Chinese greens are prepared in a very simple way – stir-fried and served with oyster sauce. The combination makes a simple, quickly prepared, tasty accompaniment.

Serves 3-4

INGREDIENTS
1 lb Chinese greens
  (*bok choy*)
2 tbsp peanut oil
1–2 tbsp oyster sauce

Chinese greens

peanut oil

oyster sauce

VARIATION
You can replace the Chinese greens with Chinese flowering cabbage, or Chinese broccoli, which is also known by its Cantonese name *choi sam*. It has green leaves and tiny yellow flowers, which are also eaten along with the leaves and stalks. It is available at Asian markets.

1 Trim the Chinese greens, removing any discolored leaves and damaged stems. Tear into manageable pieces.

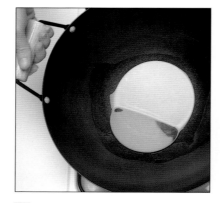

2 Heat a wok until hot, add the oil and swirl it around.

3 Add the Chinese greens and stir-fry for 2–3 minutes, until the greens have wilted a little.

4 Add the oyster sauce and continue to stir-fry a few seconds more until the greens are cooked but still slightly crisp. Serve immediately.

Fish Bites with Crispy Cabbage

Add an oriental element to a special meal with these attractive and tasty fish bites. Coated in sesame seeds and served with the traditional deep-fried cabbage, they are sure to impress.

Serves 4

INGREDIENTS
FOR THE FISH BITES
12 oz/1½ cups peeled shrimp
12 oz cod fillets
2 tsp light soy sauce
2 tsp sesame seeds
oil for deep-frying

FOR THE CABBAGE
8 oz savoy cabbage
pinch of salt
1 tbsp slivered almonds
soy sauce, to serve

sesame seeds

shrimp

soy sauce

slivered almonds

cod fillets

cabbage

1 Put the shrimp and cod in a food processor and blend for 20 seconds. Place in a bowl and stir in the soy sauce.

2 Roll the mixture into sixteen balls and toss in the sesame seeds to coat.

3 Heat the oil for deep-frying to 325°F. Shred the cabbage and place in the hot oil. Fry for 2 minutes. Drain well and keep warm. Sprinkle the cabbage with salt and toss in the almonds.

4 Fry the balls in two batches for 5 minutes until golden-brown. Remove with a draining spoon. Serve with the cabbage, and soy sauce for dipping.

Deep-fried Zucchini with Chili Sauce

Crunchy coated zucchini are great served with a fiery tomato sauce.

Serves 2

INGREDIENTS
1 tbsp olive oil
1 onion, finely chopped
1 red chili, seeded and finely diced
2 tsp hot chili powder
14 oz can chopped tomatoes
1 vegetable bouillon cube
¼ cup hot water
1 lb zucchini
⅔ cup milk
½ cup all-purpose flour
oil for deep-frying
salt and freshly ground black pepper

TO SERVE
lettuce leaves
watercress sprigs
slices of seeded bread
thyme sprigs, to garnish

zucchini

chopped tomatoes

onion

red chili

all-purpose flour

bouillon cube

milk

chili powder

1 Heat the oil in a pan. Add the onion, and cook for 2–3 minutes. Add the chili. Stir in the chili powder, and cook for 30 seconds.

2 Add the tomatoes. Crumble in the bouillon cube, and stir in the water. Cover and cook for 10 minutes.

3 Meanwhile, remove the ends from the zucchini. Cut them into ¼ in slices.

4 Pour the milk into one shallow dish, and spread out the flour in another. Dip the zucchini first in the milk, then into the flour, until well-coated.

5 Heat the oil for deep-frying to 350°F or until a cube of bread, when added to the oil, browns in 30–45 seconds. Add the zucchini slices in batches, and deep-fry for 3–4 minutes until crisp. Drain on paper towels.

6 Place two or three lettuce leaves on each serving plate. Add a few sprigs of watercress, and fan out the bread slices to one side. Season the sauce, spoon some on to each plate, top with the zucchini and garnish with the sprigs of thyme. Serve at once with a crisp salad and bread.

Masala Okra

Okra, or "ladies' fingers" are a popular Indian vegetable. In this recipe they are stir-fried with a dry, spicy masala to make a delicious side dish.

Serves 4

INGREDIENTS
1 pound okra
½ teaspoon ground turmeric
1 teaspoon cayenne pepper
1 tablespoon ground cumin
1 tablespoon ground coriander
¼ teaspoon salt
¼ teaspoon sugar
1 tablespoon lemon juice
1 tablespoon dried coconut
2 tablespoons chopped cilantro
3 tablespoons oil
½ teaspoon cumin seeds
½ teaspoon black mustard seeds
chopped fresh tomatoes, to garnish
poppadums, to serve

black mustard seeds

lemon juice

ground coriander

cumin seeds

ground cumin

cayenne pepper

sugar

okra

ground turmeric

dried coconut

salt

cilantro

COOK'S TIP
When buying okra, choose firm, brightly colored, unblemished pods that are less than 4 inches long.

1 Wash, dry and trim the okra. In a bowl, mix together the turmeric, cayenne pepper, cumin, ground coriander, salt, sugar, lemon juice, dried coconut and the cilantro.

2 Heat the oil in a large frying pan. Add the cumin seeds and mustard seeds and fry for about 2 minutes, or until they begin to sputter.

3 Add the spice mixture and continue to fry for 2 minutes.

4 Add the okra, cover, and cook over low heat for 10 minutes, or until tender. Garnish with chopped fresh tomatoes and serve with poppadums.

Cannellini Bean Purée with Broiled Radicchio

The slightly bitter flavors of the radicchio and Belgian endive make a wonderful marriage with the creamy citrus flavored bean purée.

Serves 4

INGREDIENTS
14 oz can cannellini beans
3 tbsp low-fat ricotta cheese
finely grated rind and juice of 1
  large orange
1 tbsp finely chopped fresh rosemary
4 heads of Belgian endive
2 medium radicchio
1 tbsp walnut oil

chicory

ricotta cheese

cannellini beans

rosemary

radicchio

orange

1 Drain the beans, rinse, and drain again. Purée the beans in a blender or food processor with the ricotta cheese, orange juice and rosemary. Set aside.

2 Cut the Belgian endive in half lengthwise.

3 Cut each radicchio into 8 wedges.

4 Lay out the Belgian endive and radicchio on a baking sheet. Brush with oil. Broil for 3 minutes. Serve with the sauce and orange rind.

COOK'S TIP
Other suitable beans to use are navy, mung or broad beans.

Creamy Cannellini Beans with Asparagus

Cannellini beans in a creamy sauce contrast with tender asparagus in this tasty toast topper.

Serves 2

INGREDIENTS
2 tsp butter
1 small onion, finely chopped
1 small carrot, grated
1 tsp fresh thyme leaves
14 oz can cannellini beans, drained
$^2/_3$ cup light cream
4 oz young asparagus spears, trimmed
2 slices of fresh sliced whole wheat bread
salt and freshly ground black pepper

whole wheat bread

carrot

thyme

butter

asparagus spears

light cream

onion

cannellini beans

parsley

1 Melt the butter in a pan. Add the onion and carrot, and fry over a moderate heat for 4 minutes until soft. Add the thyme leaves.

2 Rinse the cannellini beans under cold running water. Drain thoroughly. Then add to the onion and carrot. Mix lightly.

3 Pour in the cream, and heat slowly to just below boiling point, stirring occasionally. Remove the pan from the heat, and add salt and pepper to taste. Preheat the broiler.

4 Place the asparagus spears in a saucepan. Pour over just enough boiling water to cover. Poach for 3–4 minutes until the spears are just tender.

5 Meanwhile, toast the bread under the broiler until both sides are golden.

6 Place the toast on individual plates. Drain the asparagus, and divide the spears between the slices of toast. Spoon the bean mixture over each portion, and serve.

New Spring Salad

This chunky salad makes a satisfying meal. Use other spring vegetables, if you like.

Serves 4

INGREDIENTS

1½ lb small new potatoes, halved
14 oz can fava beans, drained
4 oz cherry tomatoes
½ cup walnut halves
2 tbsp white wine vinegar
1 tbsp whole-grain mustard
4 tbsp olive oil
pinch of sugar
8 oz young asparagus spears,
  trimmed
6 scallions, trimmed
salt and freshly ground black pepper
baby spinach leaves, to serve

asparagus spears

new potatoes

whole-grain mustard

fava beans

cherry tomatoes

scallions

walnut halves

1 Put the potatoes in a pan. Cover with cold water, and bring to a boil. Cook for 10–12 minutes, until tender. Meanwhile, turn the fava beans into a bowl. Cut the tomatoes in half, and add them to the bowl with the walnuts.

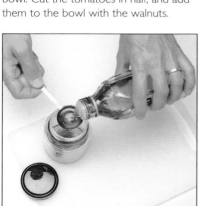

2 Put the white wine vinegar, mustard, olive oil and sugar into a jar. Add salt and pepper to taste. Close the jar tightly, and shake well.

3 Add the asparagus to the potatoes, and cook for 3 minutes more. Drain the cooked vegetables well. Cool under cold running water, and drain again. Thickly slice the potatoes, and cut the scallions into halves.

4 Add the asparagus, potatoes and scallions to the bowl containing the fava bean mixture. Pour the dressing over the salad, and toss well. Serve on a bed of baby spinach leaves.

Stir-fried Spinach with Garlic and Sesame Seeds

The sesame seeds add a crunchy texture which contrasts well with the wilted spinach in this easy vegetable dish.

Serves 2

INGREDIENTS
8 oz fresh spinach, washed
1½ tbsp sesame seeds
2 tbsp peanut oil
¼ tsp sea salt flakes
2–3 garlic cloves, sliced

spinach

peanut oil

garlic

sesame seeds

1 Shake the spinach to get rid of any excess water, then remove the stalks and discard any yellow or damaged leaves. Lay several spinach leaves one on top of another, roll up tightly and cut crossways into wide strips. Repeat with the remaining leaves.

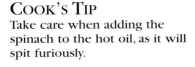

COOK'S TIP
Take care when adding the spinach to the hot oil, as it will spit furiously.

2 Heat a wok to medium heat, add the sesame seeds and dry-fry, stirring, for 1–2 minutes, until golden brown. Transfer to a small bowl and set aside.

3 Add the oil to the wok and swirl it around. When hot, add the salt, spinach and garlic and stir-fry for 2 minutes until the spinach just wilts and the leaves are coated with the oil.

4 Sprinkle over the sesame seeds and toss well. Serve at once.

Spring Vegetable Stir-fry

A colorful, dazzling medley of fresh and sweet young vegetables.

Serves 4

INGREDIENTS

1 tbsp peanut oil
1 garlic clove, sliced
1 in piece of fresh ginger root, finely chopped
4 oz baby carrots
4 oz patty pan squash
4 oz baby corn
4 oz green beans, topped and tailed
4 oz sugar-snap peas, topped and tailed
4 oz young asparagus, cut into 3 in pieces
8 scallions, trimmed and cut into 2 in pieces
4 oz cherry tomatoes

FOR THE DRESSING

juice of 2 limes
1 tbsp honey
1 tbsp soy sauce
1 tsp sesame oil

1 Heat the peanut oil in a wok or large frying pan.

2 Add the garlic and ginger and stir-fry over a high heat for 1 minute.

3 Add the carrots, patty pan squash, baby corn and beans and stir-fry for another 3–4 minutes.

4 Add the sugar-snap peas, asparagus, scallions and cherry tomatoes and stir-fry for a further 1–2 minutes.

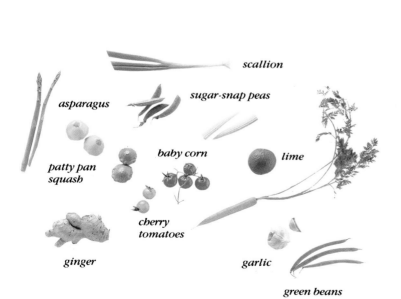

scallion

asparagus

sugar-snap peas

patty pan squash

baby corn

lime

ginger

cherry tomatoes

garlic

green beans

5 Stir in the garam masala and cumin seeds, and cook for 2 minutes.

6 Stir in the sugar and remaining spices, and cook for 1 minute or until all the liquid has evaporated.

COOK'S TIP
If ghee is not available, you can clarify your own butter. Melt ¼ cup butter slowly in a small pan. Remove from the heat, and leave for about 5 minutes. Then pour off the clear yellow clarified butter, leaving the sediment in the pan.

FISH AND SEAFOOD

Stir-fried Squid with Black Bean Sauce

If you cannot buy fresh squid you will certainly find small or baby frozen squid, skinned, boned and with heads removed, at your local fishmonger.

Serves 4

INGREDIENTS
½ lb fresh or frozen squid
1 red chili
2 tsp peanut oil
1 clove garlic, crushed
2 tbsp black bean sauce
4 tbsp water
fresh parsley sprigs, to garnish
steamed rice, to serve

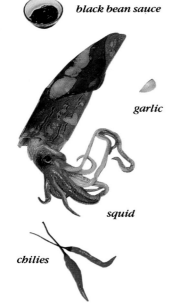

black bean sauce

garlic

squid

chilies

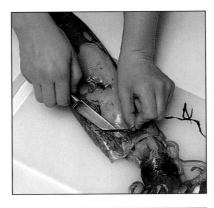

1 Carefully remove the skin from the squid and discard.

2 Cut off the head of each squid just below the eye, and discard.

3 Remove the bone from the squid and discard.

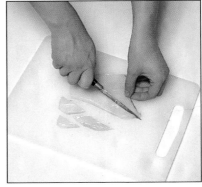

4 Cut the squid into bite-size pieces and score the flesh in a criss-cross pattern with a sharp knife.

5 Carefully deseed the chili and chop it finely. Wear rubber gloves to protect your hands if necessary.

6 Heat the wok, then add the oil. When the oil is hot, add the garlic and cook until it starts to sizzle but does not color. Stir in the squid and fry until the flesh starts to stiffen and turn white. Quickly stir in the black bean sauce, water and chili. Continue stirring until the squid is cooked and tender (not more than a minute). Garnish with parsley sprigs and the tentacles and serve with steamed rice.

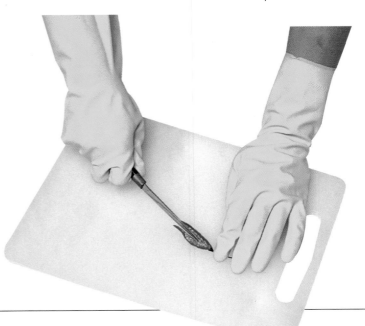

Thai Fish Stir-fry

This is a substantial dish: it is best served with chunks of fresh crusty white bread, for mopping up all the delicious, spicy juices.

Serves 4

INGREDIENTS
1 ½ lb mixed seafood (for example, red snapper, cod, raw shrimp), filleted and skinned
1 ¼ cups coconut milk
1 tbsp vegetable oil
salt and freshly ground black pepper

FOR THE SAUCE
2 large red chilies
1 onion, roughly chopped
2 in piece ginger root, peeled and sliced
2 in piece lemon grass, outer leaf discarded, roughly sliced
2 in piece galingale, peeled and sliced
6 blanched almonds, chopped
½ tsp turmeric
½ tsp salt

chili

onion

ginger

shrimp

1 Cut the filleted fish into large chunks. Peel the shrimp, keeping their tails intact.

2 Carefully remove the seeds from the chilies and chop roughly, wearing rubber gloves to protect your hands if necessary. Then, make the sauce by putting the chilies and the other sauce ingredients in the food processor with 3 tbsp of the coconut milk. Blend until smooth.

3 Heat the wok, then add the oil. When the oil is hot, stir-fry the seafood for 2–3 minutes, then remove.

4 Add the sauce and the remaining coconut milk to the wok, then return the seafood. Bring to the boil, season well and serve with crusty bread.

Cajun-style Cod

This recipe works equally well with any firm-fleshed fish such as swordfish, shark, tuna or halibut.

Serves 4

INGREDIENTS
4 cod steaks, each weighing
    about 6 oz
2 tbsp plain low fat yogurt
1 tbsp lime or lemon juice
1 garlic clove, crushed
1 tsp ground cumin
1 tsp paprika
1 tsp mustard powder
½ tsp cayenne pepper
½ tsp dried thyme
½ tsp dried oregano
baby potatoes and a mixed salad,
    to serve

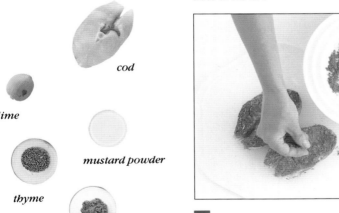

cod

lime

mustard powder

thyme

paprika

1 Pat the fish dry on absorbent paper towels. Mix together the yogurt and lime or lemon juice and brush lightly over both sides of the fish.

2 Mix together the garlic clove, spices and herbs. Coat both sides of the fish with the seasoning mix, rubbing in well.

COOK'S TIP
If you don't have a ridged broiler pan, heat several metal skewers under a broiler until red hot. Holding the ends with a cloth, press onto the seasoned fish before cooking to give a seared appearance.

3 Spray a ridged broiler pan or heavy-based frying pan with non-stick cooking spray. Heat until very hot. Add the fish and cook over a high heat for 4 minutes, or until the underside is well browned.

4 Turn over and cook for a further 4 minutes, or until the steaks have cooked through. Serve immediately accompanied with baby potatoes and a mixed salad.

Pan-fried Red Snapper with Lemon

This dish, which is spectacularly attractive and delicious, is also quick and easy to make.

Serves 4

INGREDIENTS
1 large bulb fennel
1 lemon
12 red snapper fillets, skin left intact
3 tbsp fresh marjoram, chopped
3 tbsp olive oil
8 oz/3 cups lamb's lettuce or
   Bibb lettuce
salt and freshly ground black pepper

FOR THE VINAIGRETTE
generous ¾ cup peanut oil
1 tbsp white wine vinegar
1 tbsp sherry vinegar
salt and freshly ground black pepper,
   to taste

FOR THE SAUCE
1½ oz black olives, pitted
1 tbsp unsalted butter
1 tbsp capers

fennel

red snapper

marjoram

lamb's lettuce

1 Trim the fennel bulb and cut it into fine matchsticks. Peel the lemon. Remove any excess pith from the peel, then cut it into fine strips. Blanch the rind and refresh it immediately in cold water. Drain.

2 Make the vinaigrette by placing all the ingredients in a small bowl and lightly whisking until well mixed.

3 Sprinkle the red snapper fillets with salt, pepper and marjoram.

4 Heat the wok and add the olive oil. When the oil is very hot, add the fennel and stir-fry for 1 minute, then drain and remove.

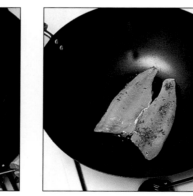

5 Reheat the wok and, when the oil is hot, stir-fry the red snapper fillets, cooking them skin-side down first for 2 minutes, then flipping them over for 1 further minute. Drain well on paper towels and wipe the wok clean with paper towels.

6 For the sauce, cut the olives into slivers. Heat the wok and add the butter. When the butter is hot, stir-fry the capers and olives for about 1 minute. Toss the lettuce in the dressing. Arrange the fillets on a bed of lettuce, topped with the fennel and lemon, and serve with the olive and caper sauce.

Jamaican Spiced Cod Steaks with Pumpkin Ragout

Spicy hot from Kingston town, this fast fish dish is guaranteed to appeal. The term 'ragout' is taken from the old French verb *ragouter*, which means to stimulate the appetite.

Serves 4

INGREDIENTS
finely grated zest of ½ orange
2 tbsp black peppercorns
1 tbsp allspice berries or Jamaican
    pepper
½ tsp salt
4 × 6 oz cod steaks
groundnut oil, for frying
new potatoes, to serve (optional)
3 tbsp chopped fresh parsley,
    to garnish

FOR THE RAGOUT
2 tbsp groundnut oil
1 medium onion, chopped
1 in fresh ginger root, peeled and
    grated
1 lb fresh pumpkin, peeled, deseeded
    and chopped
3–4 shakes of Tabasco sauce
2 tbsp soft brown sugar
1 tbsp vinegar

pumpkin

cod steaks

ginger

COOK'S TIP
This recipe can be adapted using any types of firm pink or white fish that is available, such as haddock, whiting, monkfish, halibut or tuna.

1 To make the ragout, heat the oil in a heavy saucepan and add the onion and ginger. Cover and cook, stirring, for 3–4 minutes until soft.

2 Add the chopped pumpkin, Tabasco sauce, brown sugar and vinegar, cover and cook over a low heat for 10–12 minutes until softened.

3 Combine the orange zest, peppercorns, allspice or Jamaican pepper and salt, then crush coarsely using a pestle and mortar. (Alternatively, coarsely grind the peppercorns in a pepper mill and combine with the zest and seasoning.)

4 Scatter the spice mixture over both sides of the fish and moisten with a sprinkling of oil.

5 Heat a large frying pan and fry the cod steaks for 12 minutes, turning once.

6 Serve the cod steaks with a spoonful of pumpkin ragout and new potatoes, if desired, and garnish the ragout with chopped fresh parsley.

Fish Parcels

Sea bass is good for this recipe, but you could also use small whole trout, or white fish fillet such as cod or haddock.

COOK'S TIP
These parcels can also be baked in the oven: place them on a baking sheet and cook at 400°F for 15–20 minutes.

Serves 4

4 pieces sea bass fillet or
  4 whole small sea bass,
  about 1 lb each
oil for brushing
2 shallots, thinly sliced
1 garlic clove, chopped
1 tbsp capers
6 sun-dried tomatoes, finely
  chopped
4 black olives, pitted and thinly
  sliced
grated rind and juice of
  1 lemon
1 tsp paprika
salt and freshly ground black
  pepper

1 Clean the fish if whole. Cut four large squares of double-thickness foil, large enough to enclose the fish; brush with a little oil.

2 Place a piece of fish in the center of each piece of foil and season well with salt and pepper.

3 Scatter over the shallots, garlic, capers, tomatoes, olives and grated lemon rind. Sprinkle with the lemon juice and paprika.

paprika

shallots

lemon

garlic

sun-dried tomatoes

capers

black olives

sea bass fillets

4 Fold the foil over to enclose the fish loosely, sealing the edges firmly so none of the juices can escape. Place on a moderately-hot barbecue and cook for 8–10 minutes. Then open up the tops of the parcels and serve.

Spiced Scallops in their Shells

Scallops are excellent steamed. When served with this spicy sauce, they make a delicious yet simple appetizer. Each person spoons sauce onto the scallops before eating them.

Serves 4

INGREDIENTS
8 scallops, shelled (the shells are available in cooking ware stores and some good fish markets)
2 slices fresh ginger, finely shredded
½ garlic clove, shredded
2 scallions, green parts only, shredded
salt and pepper

FOR THE SAUCE
1 garlic clove, crushed
1 tbsp fresh ginger, finely grated
2 scallions, white parts only, chopped
1–2 fresh green chilies, seeded and finely chopped
1 tbsp light soy sauce
1 tbsp dark soy sauce
2 tsp sesame oil

scallops
ginger
scallions
garlic
light soy sauce
dark soy sauce
green chili
sesame oil

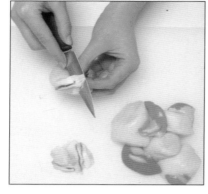

1 Remove the dark beard-like fringe and tough muscle from the scallops.

2 Place 2 scallops in each shell. Season lightly with salt and pepper, then sprinkle the ginger, garlic and scallions on top. Place the shells in a bamboo steamer and steam for about 6 minutes, until the scallops look opaque (you may have to do this in batches).

3 Meanwhile, mix together all the sauce ingredients and pour into a small serving bowl.

4 Carefully remove each shell from the steamer, taking care not to spill the juices, and arrange them on a serving plate with the sauce bowl in the center. Serve at once.

Spiced Shrimp with Coconut

This spicy dish is based on *Sambal Goreng Udang*, which is Indonesian in origin. It is best served with plain boiled rice.

Serves 3-4

INGREDIENTS
2-3 fresh red chilies, seeded
  and chopped
3 shallots, chopped
1 lemongrass stalk, chopped
2 garlic cloves, chopped
thin sliver of dried shrimp paste
½ tsp ground galangal
1 tsp ground turmeric
1 tsp ground coriander
1 tbsp peanut oil
1 cup water
2 fresh kaffir lime leaves
1 tsp light brown sugar
2 tomatoes, peeled, seeded
  and chopped
1 cup coconut milk
1½ lb large raw shrimp,
  peeled and deveined
squeeze of lemon juice
salt, to taste
shredded scallions and
  flaked coconut, to garnish

1 In a mortar pound the chilies, shallots, lemongrass, garlic, shrimp paste, galangal, turmeric and coriander with a pestle until it forms a paste.

lemongrass

garlic

dried shrimp paste

turmeric

red chilies

shrimp

coriander

peanut oil

coconut milk

sugar

galangal

tomatoes

shallots

kaffir lime leaves

COOK'S TIP
Dried shrimp paste, much used in Southeast Asia, is available at Asian stores.

2 Heat a wok until hot, add the oil and swirl it around. Add the spiced paste and stir-fry for about 2 minutes. Pour in the water and add the kaffir lime leaves, sugar and tomatoes. Simmer for 8–10 minutes, until most of the liquid has evaporated.

3 Add the coconut milk and shrimp and cook gently, stirring, for about 4 minutes until the shrimp are pink. Taste and adjust the seasoning with salt and a squeeze of lemon juice. Serve at once, garnished with shredded scallions and toasted flaked coconut.

Red Snapper with Ginger and Scallions

This is a classic Chinese way of cooking fish. Pouring the oil slowly over the scallions and ginger allows it to partially cook them, enhancing their flavor.

Serves 2-3

INGREDIENTS
1 red snapper, about
  1½-2 lb, cleaned and scaled
  with head left on
1 bunch scallions, cut into thin
  shreds
1-in piece fresh ginger, cut into
  thin shreds
¼ tsp salt
¼ tsp sugar
3 tbsp peanut oil
1 tsp sesame oil
2-3 tbsp light soy sauce
scallion brushes, to garnish

scallions

ginger

peanut oil

sesame oil

red snapper

sugar

light soy sauce

COOK'S TIP
If the fish is too big to fit inside the steamer, cut off the head and place it alongside the body, which can then be reassembled after it is cooked for serving.

1 Rinse the fish, then pat dry with paper towels. Slash the flesh diagonally, three times on each side. Set the fish on a heatproof oval plate that will fit inside your bamboo steamer.

2 Tuck about one-third of the scallions and ginger inside the body cavity. Place the plate inside the steamer, cover with its lid, then place in a wok.

3 Steam over medium heat for 10–15 minutes, until the fish flakes easily when tested with the tip of a knife.

4 Carefully remove the plate from the steamer. Sprinkle over the salt, sugar and remaining scallions and ginger.

5 Heat the oils in a small pan until very hot, then slowly pour over the fish.

6 Drizzle over the soy sauce and serve at once, garnished with scallion brushes.

Smoked Haddock Fillets with Quick Parsley Sauce

Make any herb sauce with this method, making sure it is thickened and seasoned well to complement the smoky flavor of the fish.

Serves 4

INGREDIENTS
4 × 8 oz smoked haddock fillets
6 tbsp butter, softened
2 tbsp flour
1¼ cups milk
salt and freshly ground black pepper
4 tbsp chopped fresh parsley

flour   *butter*

smoked haddock fillets

parsley

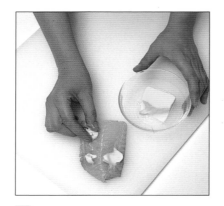

1 Smear the fish fillets liberally on both sides with 4 tbsp butter and preheat the broiler.

2 Beat the remaining butter and flour together to make a thick paste.

3 Broil the fish for 10–15 minutes turning when necessary. Meanwhile, heat the milk until just below boiling point. Add the flour mixture in small batches whisking constantly over the heat, until the sauce is smooth and thick.

4 Stir in the seasoning and parsley and serve poured over the fillets.

Thick Cod Fillet with Fresh Mixed-herb Crust

Mixed fresh herbs make this a delicious crust. Season well and serve with large lemon wedges.

Serves 4

INGREDIENTS
2 tbsp butter
1 tbsp fresh chervil
1 tbsp fresh parsley
1 tbsp fresh chives
3 cups wholewheat bread
   crumbs
4 × 8 oz thickly cut cod fillets,
   skinned
1 tbsp olive oil
lemon wedges, to garnish
salt and freshly ground black pepper

chives

butter

bread crumbs

parsley

cod fillets

chervil

lemon

1 Preheat the oven to 400°F. Melt the butter and chop the fresh herbs finely.

2 Mix the butter with the bread crumbs, herbs and seasoning.

3 Press a quarter of the mixture on top of each fillet. Place on a baking sheet and drizzle over the olive oil. Bake in the preheated oven for 15 minutes until the fish flesh is firm and the top turns golden. Serve garnished with lemon wedges.

Fillets of Pink Trout with Tarragon Cream Sauce

If you do not like the idea of cooking and serving trout on the bone, ask your fishmonger to fillet and skin the fish. Serve two fillets per person.

Serves 4

INGREDIENTS
2 tbsp butter
4 fresh trout, filleted and skinned
salt and freshly ground black pepper
new potatoes, to serve
wax beans, to serve

FOR THE CREAM SAUCE
2 large scallions, white part only,
    chopped
½ cucumber, peeled, deseeded and
    cut into short sticks
1 tsp cornstarch
⅔ cup light cream
¼ cup dry sherry
2 tbsp chopped fresh tarragon
1 tomato, chopped and deseeded

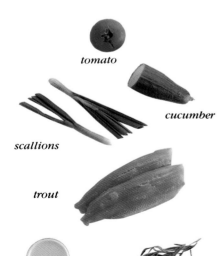

tomato

cucumber

scallions

trout

cream   tarragon

This recipe can also be made with salmon fillets and the dry sherry may be substituted with white wine.

1 Melt the butter in a large frying pan, season the fillets and cook for 6 minutes, turning once. Transfer to a plate, cover and keep warm.

2 To make the sauce, add the scallions and cucumber to the pan, and cook over a gentle heat, stirring occasionally, until soft but not colored.

3 Remove the pan from the heat and stir in the cornstarch.

4 Return to the heat and pour in the cream and sherry. Simmer to thicken, stirring continuously.

5 Add the chopped tarragon and tomato, and season to taste.

6 Spoon the sauce over the fillets and serve with buttered new potatoes and wax beans.

Sizzling Beef with Celeriac Straw

The crisp celeriac matchsticks look like fine pieces of straw when cooked and have a mild celery-like flavor that is quite delicious.

Serves 4

INGREDIENTS
1 lb celeriac
2/3 cup vegetable oil
1 red pepper
6 scallions
1 lb rump steak
4 tbsp beef stock
2 tbsp sherry vinegar
2 tsp Worcestershire sauce
2 tsp tomato paste
salt and freshly ground black pepper

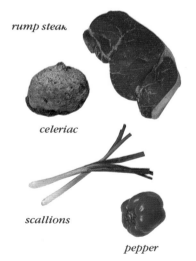

rump steak

celeriac

scallions

pepper

1 Peel the celeriac and then cut it into fine matchsticks, using a cleaver.

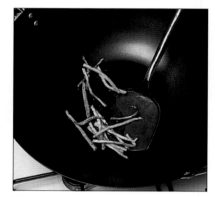

2 Heat the wok, then add two-thirds of the oil. When the oil is hot, fry the celeriac matchsticks in batches until golden brown and crispy. Drain well on paper towels.

3 Chop the red pepper and the scallions into approximate 1 in lengths, using diagonal cuts.

4 Chop the beef into strips, across the grain of the meat.

5 Heat the wok, and then add the remaining oil. When the oil is hot, stir-fry the chopped scallions and red pepper for 2–3 minutes.

6 Add the beef strips and stir-fry for a further 3—4 minutes until well browned. Add the stock, vinegar, Worcestershire sauce and tomato paste. Season well and serve with the celeriac straw.

Spicy Beef

Promoting a fast-growing trend in worldwide cuisine, the wok is used in this recipe to produce a colorful and healthy meal.

Serves 4

INGREDIENTS
1 tbsp oil
1 lb/4 cups ground beef
1 in fresh ginger root, sliced
1 tsp Chinese five-spice powder
1 red chili, sliced
2 oz snow peas
1 red bell pepper, chopped
1 carrot, sliced
4 oz beansprouts
1 tbsp sesame oil

pepper

snow peas

sesame oil

five-spice

beansprouts

ground beef

ginger

carrot

chili

1 Heat the oil in a wok until almost smoking. Add the ground beef and cook for 3 minutes, stirring all the time.

2 Add the ginger, Chinese five-spice powder and chili. Cook for 1 minute.

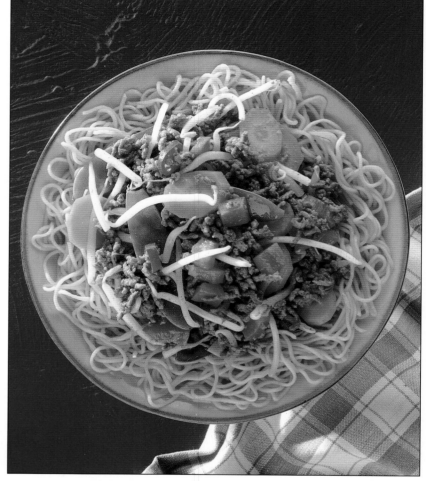

3 Add the snow peas, pepper and carrot and cook for a further 3 minutes, stirring continuously.

4 Add the beansprouts and sesame oil and cook for a final 2 minutes. Serve immediately with noodles.

Glazed Lamb

Lemon and honey make a classically good combination in sweet dishes, and this lamb recipe shows how well they work together in savory dishes, too. Serve with a fresh mixed salad to complete this delicious dish.

Serves 4

INGREDIENTS
1lb boneless lean lamb
1 tbsp grapeseed oil
6 oz snow peas, topped
  and tailed
3 scallions, sliced
2 tbsp honey
juice of half a lemon
2 tbsp fresh cilantro, chopped
1 tbsp sesame seeds
salt and freshly ground pepper

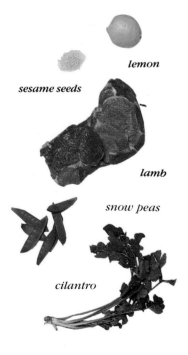

lemon

sesame seeds

lamb

snow peas

cilantro

1 Using a sharp knife, cut the lamb into thin strips.

2 Heat the wok, then add the oil. When the oil is hot, stir-fry the lamb until browned all over. Remove from the wok and keep warm.

3 Add the snow peas and sliced scallions to the hot wok and stir-fry for 30 seconds.

4 Return the lamb to the wok and add the honey, lemon juice, cilantro and sesame seeds, and season well. Bring to a boil and bubble for 1 minute until the lamb is well coated in the honey mixture.

Sukiyaki-style Beef

This Japanese dish is a meal in itself; the recipe incorporates all the traditional elements – meat, vegetables, noodles and bean curd. If you want to do it all properly, eat the meal with chopsticks, and a spoon to collect the stock juices.

Serves 4

INGREDIENTS
1 lb thick rump steak
7 oz Japanese rice noodles
1 tbsp peanut oil
7 oz firm bean curd, cut
  into cubes
8 shiitake mushrooms, trimmed
2 medium leeks, sliced into 1 in
  lengths
3½ oz baby spinach, well washed,
  to serve

FOR THE STOCK
1 tbsp superfine sugar
6 tbsp rice wine
3 tbsp dark soy sauce
½ cup water

rice noodles

leek

baby spinach

shiitake mushrooms

rump steak

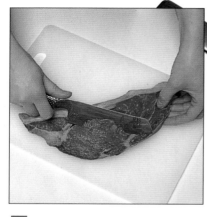

1 Cut the beef into thin slices.

2 Blanch the noodles in boiling water for 2 minutes. Strain well.

3 Mix together all the stock ingredients in a bowl.

4 Heat the wok, then add the oil. When the oil is hot, stir-fry the beef for about 2–3 minutes, until it is cooked but still pink in color.

5 Pour the stock over the beef.

6 Add the remaining ingredients and cook for 4 minutes, until the leeks are tender. Serve a selection of the different ingredients, with a few baby spinach leaves, to each person.

Veal Escalopes with Artichokes

Artichokes are very hard to prepare fresh, so use canned artichoke hearts, instead – they have an excellent flavor and are simple to use.

Serves 4

INGREDIENTS
1 lb veal escalopes
1 shallot
4 oz lean smoked bacon, finely
   chopped
1 × 14 oz can of artichoke hearts in
   brine, drained and quartered
2/3 cup veal stock
3 fresh rosemary sprigs
4 tbsp heavy cream
salt and freshly ground black pepper
fresh rosemary sprigs, to garnish

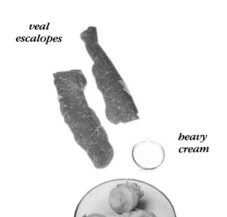

veal escalopes

heavy cream

artichoke hearts

1 Cut the veal into thin slices.

2 Using a sharp knife, cut the shallot into thin slices.

3 Heat the wok, then add the bacon. Stir-fry for 2 minutes. When the fat is released, add the veal and shallot and stir-fry for 3–4 minutes.

4 Add the artichokes and stir-fry for 1 minute. Stir in the stock and rosemary and simmer for 2 minutes. Stir in the heavy cream, season with salt and pepper and serve immediately, garnished with sprigs of fresh rosemary.

Chicken Liver Kebabs

These may be barbecued outdoors and served with salad and baked potatoes, or broiled indoors and served with rice and broccoli.

Serves 4

INGREDIENTS
4 oz (roughly 6) lean bacon rashers
12 oz trimmed chicken livers
12 large, ready-to-eat pitted prunes
12 cherry tomatoes
8 button mushrooms
2 tbsp olive oil

prunes
olive oil
tomatoes
mushrooms
bacon

chicken livers

1 Cut each rasher of bacon into two pieces, wrap a piece around each chicken liver and secure in position with wooden toothpicks.

2 Wrap the pitted prunes around the cherry tomatoes.

3 Thread the bacon-wrapped livers onto metal skewers with the tomatoes and prunes. Brush with oil. Cover the tomatoes and prunes with foil to protect them while broiling or barbecuing. Cook for 5 minutes on each side.

4 Remove the toothpicks and serve the kebabs immediately.

Pan-fried Pork with Peaches and Green Peppercorns

When peaches are in season, consider this speedy pork dish, brought alive with green peppercorns.

Serves 4

INGREDIENTS

2 cups long-grain rice
4 cups chicken stock
4 × 7 oz pork chops or
  loin pieces
2 tbsp vegetable oil
2 tbsp dark rum or sherry
1 small onion, chopped
3 large ripe peaches
1 tbsp green peppercorns
1 tbsp white wine vinegar
salt and freshly ground black pepper

onion

pork chops

dark rum

oil

green peppercorns

white wine vinegar

peaches

1 Cover the rice with 3¾ cups chicken stock. Stir, bring to a simmer and cook uncovered for 15 minutes. Switch off the heat and cover for 5 minutes. Season the pork with a generous twist of black pepper. Heat a large bare metal frying pan and moisten the pork with 1 tbsp of the oil. Cook the pork for 12 minutes, turning once.

4 Cover the peaches with boiling water to loosen the skins, then peel, slice and discard the pits.

2 Transfer the meat to a warm plate. Pour off the excess fat from the pan and return to the heat. Allow the sediment to sizzle and brown, add the rum or sherry and loosen the sediment with a flat wooden spoon. Pour the pan contents over the meat, cover and keep warm. Wipe the pan clean.

5 Add the peaches and peppercorns to the onion and coat for 3–4 minutes, until they begin to soften.

VARIATION

If peaches are not ripe when picked, they can be difficult to peel. Only tree ripened fruit is suitable for peeling. If fresh peaches are out of season, a can of sliced peaches may be used instead.

3 Heat the remaining vegetable oil in the pan and soften the onion over a steady heat.

6 Add the remaining chicken stock and simmer briefly. Return the pork and meat juices to the pan, sharpen with vinegar, and season to taste. Serve with the rice.

Wild Mushroom Rösti with Bacon and Eggs

Dried ceps or porcini mushrooms, commonly found in Italian delicatessens, are a good substitute for fresh. Cook them in a potato rösti and serve with bacon and a fried egg for breakfast or a lazy supper.

Serves 4

INGREDIENTS
1½ lb baking potatoes, peeled
¼ oz dried ceps or porcini
   mushrooms
2 fresh thyme sprigs, chopped
2 tbsp chopped fresh parsley
4 tbsp vegetable oil, for frying
4 × 4 oz unsmoked bacon
pinch of salt
4 eggs, to serve
1 bunch watercress or flat-leaf parsley,
   to serve

bacon

thyme

parsley

potatoes

dried ceps

watercress

eggs

COOK'S TIP
A large rösti can be made in a non-stick frying pan. Allow 12 minutes to cook. Half-way through the cooking time, invert the rösti on a large plate and slide back into the pan.

1 Bring the potatoes to a boil in a pan of salted water and cook for 5 minutes.

2 Cover the mushrooms with boiling water to soften, then chop roughly.

3 Drain the potatoes, allow them to cool and grate them coarsely. Add the mushrooms, thyme and parsley and combine together well.

4 Heat 2 tbsp of the oil in a frying pan, spoon in the rösti mixture in heaps and flatten. Fry for 6 minutes, turning once during cooking.

5 Preheat a moderate broiler and cook the bacon slices until sizzling.

6 Heat the remaining oil in a frying pan and fry the eggs as you like them. Serve the rösti together with the eggs and bacon and a watercress salad.

Stir-fried Pork with Mustard

Fry the apples for this dish very carefully, because they will disintegrate if they are overcooked.

Serves 4

INGREDIENTS
1¼ lb pork fillet
1 tart apple, such as Granny Smith
3 tbsp unsalted butter
1 tbsp superfine sugar
1 small onion, finely chopped
2 tbsp Calvados, Applejack or
    other brandy
1 tbsp Meaux or coarse-grain
    mustard
⅔ cup heavy cream
2 tbsp fresh parsley, chopped
salt and freshly ground black pepper
flat-leaf parsley sprigs, to garnish

pork fillet

onion

mustard

apple

1 Cut the pork fillet into thin slices.

2 Peel and core the apple. Cut it into thick slices.

3 Heat the wok, then add half the butter. When the butter is hot, add the apple slices, sprinkle over the sugar, and stir-fry for 2–3 minutes. Remove the apple and set aside. Wipe out the wok with paper towels.

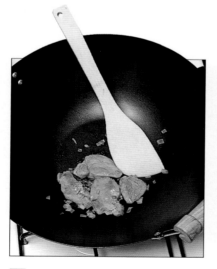

4 Heat the wok, then add the remaining butter and stir-fry the pork fillet and onion together for 2–3 minutes, until the pork is golden and the onion has begun to soften.

5 Stir in the Calvados, Applejack or other brandy and boil until it is reduced by half. Stir in the mustard.

6 Add the cream and simmer for 1 minute, then stir in the parsley. Serve garnished with sprigs of flat-leaf parsley.

Chinese Duck in Pita

This recipe is based on Chinese crispy duck but uses duck breast instead of whole duck. After 15 minutes cooking, the duck breast will still have a pinkish tinge. If you like it well-done, leave it in the oven for about 5 minutes more.

Makes 2

INGREDIENTS
1 duck breast, weighing about 6 oz
3 scallions
3 in piece hothouse cucumber
2 round pita breads
2 tbsp hoi-sin sauce
radish chrysanthemum and scallion
   tassel, to garnish

pita breads

cucumber

duck breast

hoi-sin sauce

scallions

1 Preheat the oven to 425°F. Skin the duck breast, place the skin and breast separately on a rack, and cook in the oven for 10 minutes.

2 Remove the skin from the oven, cut into pieces, and return to the oven for 5 minutes more.

3 Meanwhile, cut the scallions and cucumber into fine shreds about 1 ½ in long.

4 Heat the pita bread in the oven for a few minutes until puffed up, then split in half to make a pocket.

5 Slice the duck breast thinly.

6 Stuff the duck breast into the pita bread with a little scallion, cucumber, crispy duck skin, and some hoi-sin sauce. Serve garnished with a radish chrysanthemum and scallion tassel.

Stir-fried Turkey with Broccoli and Mushrooms

This is a really easy, tasty supper dish which works well with chicken too.

Serves 4

INGREDIENTS
4 oz broccoli florets
4 scallions
1 tsp cornstarch
3 tbsp oyster sauce
1 tbsp dark soy sauce
½ cup chicken stock,
   or bouillon cube
   and water
2 tsp lemon juice
3 tbsp peanut oil
1 lb turkey fillets, cut into
   strips, about ¼ x 2 in
1 small onion, chopped
2 garlic cloves, crushed
2 tsp fresh ginger,
   finely grated
4 oz fresh shiitake
   mushrooms, sliced
3 oz canned baby corn,
   halved lengthwise
1 tbsp sesame oil
salt and ground black pepper
egg noodles, to serve

1 Divide the broccoli florets into smaller sprigs and cut the stalks into thin diagonal slices.

2 Finely chop the white parts of the scallions and slice the green parts into thin shreds.

onion

broccoli

scallion

oyster sauce   *turkey*   *mushrooms*

lemon

dark soy sauce

baby corn

peanut oil

garlic

chicken stock

3 In a bowl, blend together the cornstarch, oyster sauce, soy sauce, stock and lemon juice. Set aside.

4 Heat a wok until hot, add 2 tbsp of the peanut oil and swirl it around. Add the turkey and stir-fry for about 2 minutes, until golden and crispy at the edges. Remove the turkey from the wok and keep warm.

5 Add the remaining peanut oil to the wok and stir-fry the chopped onion, garlic and ginger over medium heat for about 1 minute. Increase the heat to high, add the broccoli, mushrooms and corn and stir-fry for 2 minutes.

6 Return the turkey to the wok, then add the sauce with the chopped scallion and seasoning. Cook, stirring, for about 1 minute, until the sauce has thickened. Then stir in the sesame oil. Serve immediately on a bed of egg noodles with the finely shredded scallion sprinkled on top.

Chicken Liver Stir-fry

The final sprinkling of lemon, parsley and garlic granita gives this dish a delightful fresh flavor and wonderful aroma.

Serves 4

INGREDIENTS
1¼ lb chicken livers
6 tbsp butter
6 oz field mushrooms
2 oz chanterelle mushrooms
3 cloves garlic, finely chopped
2 shallots, finely chopped
⅔ cup medium sherry
3 fresh rosemary sprigs
2 tbsp fresh parsley, chopped
rind of 1 lemon, grated
salt and freshly ground pepper
fresh rosemary sprigs, to garnish
4 thick slices of white toast, to serve

1 Clean and trim the chicken livers to remove any gristle or muscle.

2 Season the livers generously with salt and freshly ground black pepper, tossing well to coat thoroughly.

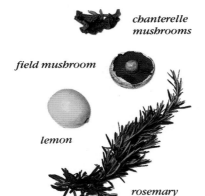

chanterelle mushrooms

field mushroom

lemon

rosemary

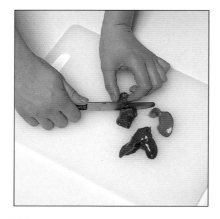

3 Heat the wok and add 1 tbsp of the butter. When melted, add the livers in batches (melting more butter where necessary but reserving 2 tbsp for the vegetables) and flash-fry until golden brown. Drain with a slotted spoon and transfer to a plate, then place in a low oven to keep warm.

4 Cut the field mushrooms into thick slices and, depending on the size of the chanterelles, cut in half.

5 Heat the wok and add the remaining butter. When melted, stir in two-thirds of the chopped garlic and the shallots and stir-fry for 1 minute until golden brown. Stir in the mushrooms and continue to cook for a further 2 minutes.

6 Add the sherry, bring to a boil and simmer for 2–3 minutes until syrupy. Add the rosemary, salt and pepper and return livers to the pan. Stir-fry for 1 minute. Garnish with extra sprigs of rosemary, and serve sprinkled with a mixture of lemon, parsley and the remaining chopped garlic, with slices of toast.

Indonesian-style Satay Chicken

Use boneless chicken thighs to give a good flavor to these satays.

Serves 4

INGREDIENTS
½ cup raw peanuts
3 tbsp vegetable oil
1 small onion, finely chopped
1 in piece ginger root, peeled and finely chopped
1 clove garlic, crushed
1½ lb chicken thighs, skinned and cut into cubes
3½ oz creamed coconut, chopped
1 tbsp chili sauce
4 tbsp chunky peanut butter
1 tsp soft dark brown sugar
⅔ cup milk
¼ tsp salt

COOK'S TIP
Soak bamboo skewers in cold water for at least 2 hours, or preferably overnight, so they do not char when keeping the threaded chicken warm in the oven.

1 Shell and rub the skins from the peanuts, then soak them in enough water to cover, for 1 minute. Drain the nuts and cut them into slivers.

2 Heat the wok and add 1 tsp oil. When the oil is hot, stir-fry the peanuts for 1 minute until crisp and golden. Remove with a slotted spoon and drain on paper towels.

3 Add the remaining oil to the hot wok. When the oil is hot, add the onion, ginger and garlic and stir-fry for 2–3 minutes until softened but not browned. Remove with a slotted spoon and drain on paper towels.

4 Add the chicken pieces and stir-fry for 3–4 minutes until crisp and golden on all sides. Thread on to pre-soaked bamboo skewers and keep warm.

creamed coconut

peanuts

chili sauce

peanut butter

5 Add the creamed coconut to the hot wok in small pieces and stir-fry until melted. Add the chili sauce, peanut butter and cooked ginger and garlic, and simmer for 2 minutes. Stir in the sugar, milk and salt, and simmer for a further 3 minutes. Serve the skewered chicken hot, with a dish of the hot dipping sauce sprinkled with the roasted peanuts.

Glazed Chicken with Cashew Nuts

Hoisin sauce lends a sweet yet slightly hot note to this chicken dish, while cashew nuts add a pleasing contrast of texture.

Serves 4

INGREDIENTS
¾ cup cashew nuts
1 red bell pepper
1 lb skinless and boneless
   chicken breasts
3 tbsp peanut oil
4 garlic cloves, finely chopped
2 tbsp Chinese rice wine or
   medium-dry sherry
3 tbsp hoisin sauce
2 tsp sesame oil
5–6 scallions,
   green parts only,
   cut into 1-in lengths

scallions

chicken

red pepper

cashew nuts

Chinese rice wine

garlic

peanut oil

hoisin sauce

sesame oil

1 Heat a wok until hot, add the cashew nuts and stir-fry over low to medium heat for 1–2 minutes, until golden brown. Remove and set aside.

3 Heat the wok again until hot, add the oil and swirl it around. Add the garlic and let it sizzle in the oil for a few seconds. Add the pepper and chicken and stir-fry for 2 minutes.

2 Halve the pepper and remove the seeds. Slice the pepper and chicken into finger-length strips.

4 Add the rice wine or sherry and hoisin sauce. Continue to stir-fry until the chicken is tender and all the ingredients are evenly glazed.

VARIATION
Use blanched almonds instead of cashew nuts if you prefer.

5 Stir in the sesame oil, toasted cashew nuts and scallion tips. Serve immediately with rice or noodles.

Caesar Salad

There are many stories about the origin of Caesar Salad. The most likely is that it was invented by an Italian, Caesar Cardini, who owned a restaurant in Mexico in the 1920s. Simplicity is the key to its success.

Serves 4

INGREDIENTS
3 slices day-old bread, ½ in thick
4 tbsp garlic oil
salt and pepper
2 oz piece Parmesan cheese
1 romaine lettuce

DRESSING
2 egg yolks, as fresh as possible
1 oz canned anchovies, roughly chopped
½ tsp Dijon mustard
½ cup olive oil, preferably Italian
1 tbsp white-wine vinegar

COOK'S TIP

The classic dressing for Caesar Salad is made with raw egg yolks. Ensure you use only the freshest eggs, bought from a reputable dealer. Expectant mothers, young children and the elderly are not advised to eat raw egg yolks. You could omit them from the dressing and grate hard-cooked yolks on top of the salad instead.

1 To make the dressing, combine the egg yolks, anchovies, mustard, oil, and vinegar in a screw-top jar and shake well.

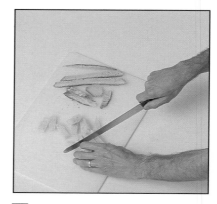

2 Remove the crusts from the bread with a serrated knife and cut into 1 in fingers.

3 Heat the garlic oil in a large skillet, add the pieces of bread, and fry until golden. Sprinkle with salt and leave to drain on paper towels.

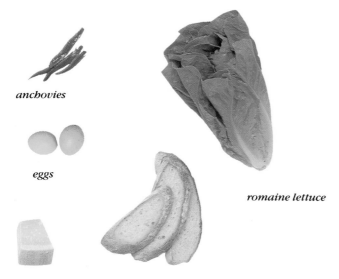

anchovies

eggs

romaine lettuce

Parmesan cheese

bread

4 Cut thin shavings from the Parmesan cheese with a vegetable peeler.

5 Wash the salad leaves and spin dry. Smother with the dressing, and scatter with garlic croutons and Parmesan cheese. Season and serve.

Arugula, Pear, and Parmesan Salad

For a sophisticated start to an elaborate meal, try this simple salad of honey-rich pears, fresh Parmesan, and aromatic leaves of arugula. Enjoy with a young Beaujolais or chilled Lambrusco wine.

Serves 4

INGREDIENTS
3 ripe pears, Williams or Packhams
2 tsp lemon juice
3 tbsp hazelnut or walnut oil
4 oz arugula
3 oz Parmesan cheese
black pepper
open-textured bread, to serve

arugula

Parmesan cheese

pears

1 Peel and core the pears and slice thickly. Toss with lemon juice to keep the flesh white.

2 Combine the nut oil with the pears. Add the arugula leaves and toss.

3 Transfer the salad to 4 small plates and top with shavings of Parmesan cheese. Season with freshly ground black pepper and serve.

COOK'S TIP

If you are unable to buy arugula easily, you can grow your own from early spring to late summer.

Melon and Prosciutto Salad with Strawberry Salsa

Sections of cool fragrant melon wrapped with slices of air-dried ham make a delicious salad starter. If strawberries are in season, serve with a savory-sweet strawberry salsa and watch it disappear.

Serves 4

INGREDIENTS

1 large melon, cantaloupe, Spanish or charentais
6 oz prosciutto, thinly sliced

SALSA

½ lb strawberries
1 tsp superfine sugar
2 tbsp peanut or sunflower oil
1 tbsp orange juice
½ tsp finely grated orange zest
½ tsp finely grated fresh ginger
salt and black pepper

2 To make the salsa, hull the strawberries and cut them into large dice. Place in a small mixing bowl with the sugar and crush lightly to release the juices. Add the oil, orange juice, zest, and ginger. Season with salt and a generous twist of black pepper.

3 Arrange the melon on a serving plate, lay the ham over the top, and serve with a bowl of salsa.

1 Halve the melon and take the seeds out with a spoon. Cut the rind away with a paring knife, then slice the melon thickly. Chill until ready to serve.

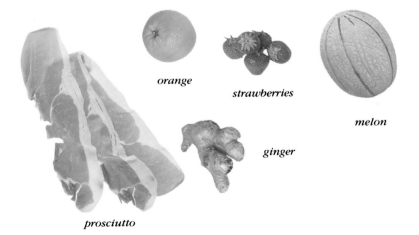

orange

strawberries

melon

ginger

prosciutto

Chicken Liver Salad

This salad may be served as a first course on individual plates.

Serves 4

INGREDIENTS
mixed salad leaves, e.g. frisée and
    oakleaf lettuce or radicchio
1 avocado, diced
2 pink grapefruits, segmented
12 oz trimmed chicken livers
2 tbsp olive oil
1 garlic clove, crushed
salt and freshly ground black pepper
crusty bread, to serve

FOR THE DRESSING
2 tbsp lemon juice
4 tbsp olive oil
½ tsp whole grain mustard
½ tsp honey
1 tbsp snipped fresh chives

chicken livers

grapefruit

olive oil

honey

avocado

mustard

lemon

chives

salad leaves

garlic

1 First prepare the dressing: put all the ingredients into a screw-topped jar and shake vigorously to emulsify. Taste and adjust the seasoning.

2 Wash and dry the salad. Arrange attractively on a serving plate with the avocado and grapefruit.

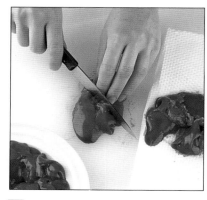

3 Dry the chicken livers on paper towels and remove any unwanted pieces. Cut the larger livers in half and leave the smaller ones whole.

4 Heat the oil in a large frying pan. Stir-fry the livers and garlic briskly until the livers are brown all over (they should be slightly pink inside).

5 Season with salt and freshly ground black pepper and drain on paper towels.

6 Place the liver on the salad and spoon over the dressing. Serve immediately with warm crusty bread.

Fresh Spinach and Avocado Salad

Young, tender spinach leaves make a change from lettuce and are delicious served with avocado, cherry tomatoes and radishes in a tofu sauce.

Serves 2–3

INGREDIENTS
1 large avocado
juice of 1 lime
8 oz fresh baby spinach leaves
4 oz cherry tomatoes
4 scallions, sliced
¹/₂ cucumber
2 oz radishes, sliced

FOR THE DRESSING
4 oz soft silken tofu
3 tbsp milk
2 tsp prepared mustard
¹/₂ tsp white wine vinegar
pinch of cayenne
salt and freshly ground black pepper

tofu *scallions*

spinach leaves

cherry tomatoes

avocado

white wine vinegar

mustard

cayenne *lime*

cucumber

radishes

milk

1 Cut the avocado in half, remove the pit, and strip off the skin. Cut the flesh into slices. Transfer to a plate, drizzle over the lime juice, and set aside.

2 Wash and dry the spinach leaves. Put them in a mixing bowl.

COOK'S TIP
Use soft silken tofu rather than the block variety. It can be found in most supermarkets in the vegetable or refrigerated sections.

3 Cut the larger cherry tomatoes in half, and add all the tomatoes to the mixing bowl, with the scallions. Cut the cucumber into chunks, and add to the bowl with the sliced radishes.

4 Make the dressing. Put the tofu, milk, mustard, wine vinegar and cayenne in a food processor or blender. Add salt and pepper to taste. Process for 30 seconds until smooth. Scrape the dressing into a bowl, and add a little extra milk if you like a thinner dressing. Sprinkle with a little extra cayenne, and garnish with radish roses and herb sprigs, if desired.

Roquefort and Walnut Pasta Salad

This is a simple earthy salad, relying totally on the quality of the ingredients. There is no real substitute for the Roquefort – a blue-veined ewe's-milk cheese from southwestern France.

Serves 4

INGREDIENTS
½ lb pasta shapes
selection of salad leaves (such as arugula, frisée, lamb's lettuce, baby spinach, radicchio, etc.)
2 tbsp walnut oil
4 tbsp sunflower oil
2 tbsp red-wine vinegar or sherry vinegar
salt and pepper
½ lb Roquefort cheese, roughly crumbled
1 cup walnut halves

pasta shapes

Roquefort cheese   *walnuts*

salad leaves

COOK'S TIP
Try toasting the walnuts under the broiler for a couple of minutes to release the flavor.

1 Cook the pasta in plenty of boiling salted water according to the manufacturer's instructions. Drain well and cool. Wash and dry the salad leaves and place in a bowl.

2 Whisk together the walnut oil, sunflower oil, vinegar, and salt and pepper to taste.

3 Pile the pasta in the center of the leaves, scatter over the crumbled Roquefort, and pour over the dressing.

4 Scatter over the walnuts. Toss just before serving.

Shrimp and Mint Salad

Shrimp make all the difference to this salad, as the flavors marinate well into the shrimp before cooking. Garnish with shavings of fresh coconut for a tropical topping.

Serves 4

INGREDIENTS
12 large shrimp
1 tbsp unsalted butter
1 tbsp fish sauce
juice of 1 lime
3 tbsp thin coconut milk
1 tsp sugar
1 garlic clove, crushed
1 in piece of ginger root, peeled and grated
2 fresh red chilies, seeded and finely chopped
freshly ground black pepper
2 tbsp fresh mint leaves
½ head light green lettuce leaves, to serve

lime

red chili

shrimp

fish sauce

coconut milk

mint

ginger   *lettuce*

1 Peel the shrimp leaving the tails intact.

2 Remove the vein.

3 Melt the butter in a large frying pan and toss in the shrimp until they turn pink.

4 Mix the fish sauce, lime juice, coconut milk, sugar, garlic, ginger, chilies and pepper together.

5 Toss the warm shrimp into the sauce with the mint leaves. Serve the shrimp mixture on a bed of green lettuce leaves.

VARIATION
The shrimp can be substituted with lobster tails if you are feeling extravagant.

Tomato and Feta Cheese Salad

Sweet sun-ripened tomatoes are rarely more delicious than when served with feta cheese and olive oil. This salad, popular in Greece and Turkey, is enjoyed as a light meal with pieces of crispy bread.

Serves 4

INGREDIENTS
2 lb tomatoes
7 oz feta cheese
½ cup olive oil, preferably Greek
12 black olives
4 sprigs fresh basil
black pepper

COOK'S TIP
Feta cheese has a strong flavor and can be salty. The least salty variety is imported from Greece and Turkey, and is available from specialty or gourmet stores.

tomatoes

basil

feta cheese

olives

2 Slice the tomatoes thickly and arrange in a shallow dish.

3 Crumble the cheese over the tomatoes, sprinkle with olive oil, then sprinkle over the olives and fresh basil. Season with freshly ground black pepper and serve at room temperature.

1 Remove the tough cores from the tomatoes with a small knife.

Tuna Fish and Flageolet Bean Salad

Two cans of tuna fish form the basis of this delicious store cupboard salad.

Serves 4

INGREDIENTS
6 tbsp mayonnaise
1 tsp mustard
2 tbsp capers
3 tbsp chopped fresh parsley
pinch of celery salt
2 × 7 oz cans tuna fish in oil, drained
3 Bibb lettuces
1 × 14 oz can flageolet beans, drained
1 × 14 oz can baby artichoke hearts, halved
12 cherry tomatoes, halved
toasted sesame bread, to serve

tomatoes

parsley

Bibb lettuce

artichoke hearts

mustard

capers

tuna fish

flageolet beans

1 Combine the mayonnaise, mustard, capers and parsley in a mixing bowl. Season to taste with celery salt. Flake the tuna into the dressing and toss gently.

2 Arrange the lettuce leaves on four plates, then spoon the tuna mixture onto the leaves.

3 Spoon the flageolet beans to one side, followed by the tomatoes and artichoke hearts. Serve with slices of toasted sesame bread.

VARIATION
Flageolet beans are taken from the under-developed pods of navy beans. They have a sweet creamy flavor and an attractive green color. If not available, use cannellini beans.

Zucchini Puffs with Salad and Balsamic Dressing

This unusual salad consists of deep-fried zucchini, flavored with mint, and served warm on a bed of salad leaves with a balsamic dressing.

Serves 2

INGREDIENTS
1 lb zucchini
1¹/₂ cups fresh white bread crumbs
1 egg
pinch of cayenne pepper
1 tbsp chopped fresh mint
oil for deep-frying
3 tbsp balsamic vinegar
3 tbsp extra virgin olive oil
7 oz mixed salad leaves
salt and freshly ground black pepper

zucchini

white bread crumbs

balsamic vinegar

mixed salad leaves

egg

mint

1 Remove the ends from the zucchini. Coarsely grate them, and put into a colander. Squeeze out the excess water. Then put the zucchini into a bowl.

2 Add the bread crumbs, egg, cayenne, mint and seasoning. Mix well.

3 Shape the zucchini mixture into balls, about the size of walnuts.

4 Heat the oil for deep-frying to 350°F or until a cube of bread, when added to the oil, browns in 30–40 seconds. Deep-fry the zucchini balls in batches for 2–3 minutes. Drain on paper towels.

5 Whisk the vinegar and oil together, and season well.

6 Put the salad leaves in a bowl, and pour over the dressing. Add the zucchini puffs, and toss lightly together. Serve at once, while the puffs are still crisp.

Belgian Endive, Fruit and Nut Salad

Mildly bitter endive is wonderful with sweet fruit, and is especially delicious when complemented by a creamy curry sauce.

Serves 4

INGREDIENTS
3 tbsp mayonnaise
1 tbsp strained, plain yogurt
1 tbsp mild curry paste
6 tbsp light cream
$^{1}/_{2}$ iceberg lettuce
2 heads of Belgian endive
$^{1}/_{2}$ cup cashews
$1^{1}/_{4}$ cups flaked coconut
2 red apples
$^{1}/_{2}$ cup currants

currants

iceberg lettuce

cashews

curry paste

mayonnaise

red apples

light cream

flaked coconut

Belgian endive

1 Mix the mayonnaise, yogurt, curry paste and light cream in a small bowl. Cover, and chill until required.

2 Tear the iceberg lettuce into pieces, and put into a salad bowl.

3 Cut the root end off each head of Belgian endive, and discard. Slice the endive, and add it to the salad bowl.

4 Preheat the broiler. Toast the cashews for 2 minutes until they are golden. Turn into a bowl, and set aside. Spread out the coconut flakes on a baking sheet. Broil for 1 minute.

5 Quarter the apples, and cut out the cores. Slice the apples, and add to the lettuce with the cashews, flaked coconut, and currants.

COOK'S TIP
Watch the coconut and cashews very carefully when broiling, as they brown very fast.

6 Spoon the dressing over the salad. Toss lightly, and serve.

Chicken and Pasta Salad

This is a delicious way to use up left-over cooked chicken, and makes a filling meal.

Serves 4

INGREDIENTS
8 oz tri-colored pasta twists
2 tbsp bottied pesto sauce
1 tbsp olive oil
1 beefsteak tomato
12 pitted black olives
8 oz cooked green beans
12 oz cooked chicken, cubed
salt and freshly ground black pepper
fresh basil, to garnish

tomato

pesto sauce

green beans

basil

olive oil

pasta twists

chicken

black olives

1 Cook the pasta in plenty of boiling, salted water until *al dente* (for about 12 minutes or as directed on the package).

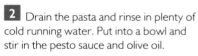

2 Drain the pasta and rinse in plenty of cold running water. Put into a bowl and stir in the pesto sauce and olive oil.

3 Skin the tomato by placing in boiling water for about 10 seconds and then into cold water, to loosen the skin.

4 Cut the tomato into small cubes and add to the pasta with the black olives, seasoning and green beans cut into 1 ½ in lengths. Add the cubed chicken. Toss gently together and transfer to a serving platter. Garnish with fresh basil.

Poor Boy Steak Salad

'Poor Boy' started life in the Italian Creole community of New Orleans when the poor survived on sandwiches filled with leftover scraps. Times have improved since then, and today the 'Poor Boy' sandwich is commonly filled with tender beef strips and other goodies. This is a salad version of 'Poor Boy'.

Serves 4

INGREDIENTS
4 sirloin or rump steaks, each
   weighing 6 oz
1 escarole lettuce
1 bunch watercress
4 tomatoes, quartered
4 large dill pickles, sliced
4 scallions, sliced
4 canned artichoke hearts, halved
6 oz button mushrooms, sliced
12 green olives
½ cup French Dressing
salt and black pepper

1 Season the steaks with black pepper. Cook the steaks under a moderate broiler for 6–8 minutes, turning once, until medium-rare. Cover and leave to rest in a warm place.

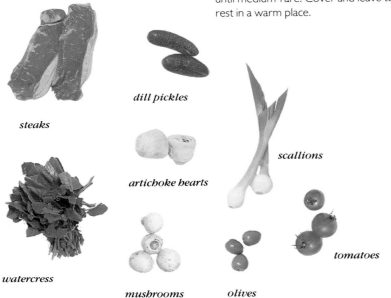

steaks

dill pickles

artichoke hearts

scallions

watercress

mushrooms

olives

tomatoes

2 Wash the salad leaves and spin dry. Combine with the remainder of the ingredients (except the steak) and toss with the French Dressing.

3 Divide the salad between 4 plates. Slice each steak diagonally and position over the salad. Season with salt and serve.

Avocado, Tomato, and Mozzarella Pasta Salad with Pine Nuts

A salad made from ingredients representing the colors of the Italian flag – a sunny cheerful dish!

Serves 4

INGREDIENTS
1½ cups pasta bows (farfalle)
6 ripe red tomatoes
½ lb mozzarella cheese
1 large ripe avocado
2 tbsp pine nuts, toasted
1 sprig fresh basil, to garnish

DRESSING
6 tbsp olive oil
2 tbsp wine vinegar
1 tsp balsamic vinegar (optional)
1 tsp whole-grain mustard
pinch of sugar
salt and pepper
2 tbsp chopped fresh basil

olive oil
avocado
tomatoes
basil
mozzarella cheese
pine nuts *pasta bows*

1 Cook the pasta in plenty of boiling salted water according to the manufacturer's instructions. Drain well and cool.

2 Slice the tomatoes and mozzarella cheese into thin rounds.

3 Halve the avocado, remove the pit, and peel off the skin. Slice the flesh lengthwise.

4 Whisk all the dressing ingredients together in a small bowl.

5 Arrange the tomato, mozzarella, and avocado in overlapping slices around the edge of a flat plate.

6 Toss the pasta with half the dressing and the chopped basil. Pile into the center of the plate. Pour over the remaining dressing, scatter over the pine nuts, and garnish with a sprig of fresh basil. Serve immediately.

Thai Seafood Salad

This seafood salad with chili, lemongrass and fish sauce is light and refreshing.

Serves 4

INGREDIENTS
8 oz cleaned squid
8 oz raw large shrimp
8 sea scallops, whole
8 oz firm white fish
2–3 tbsp olive oil
small mixed lettuce leaves and
    cilantro sprigs, to serve

FOR THE DRESSING
2 small fresh red chilies, seeded
    and finely chopped
2-in piece lemongrass,
    finely chopped
2 fresh kaffir lime leaves,
    shredded
2 tbsp Thai fish sauce
    (*nam pla*)
2 shallots, thinly sliced
2 tbsp lime juice
2 tbsp rice vinegar
2 tsp sugar

white fish   *squid*

scallops

large shrimp

lemongrass

Thai fish sauce

shallots   *kaffir lime leaves*

1 Prepare the seafood: slit open the squid bodies, score the flesh with a sharp knife, then cut into square pieces. Halve the tentacles, if necessary. Peel and devein the shrimp. Cut the sea scallops in half (if using bay scallops, leave whole). Cube the white fish.

2 Heat a wok until hot. Add the oil and swirl it around, then add the shrimp and stir-fry for 2–3 minutes until pink. Transfer to a large bowl. Stir-fry the squid and scallops for 1–2 minutes, until opaque. Remove and add to the shrimp. Stir-fry the white fish for 2–3 minutes. Remove and add to the cooked seafood. Reserve any juices.

3 Put all the dressing ingredients in a small bowl with the reserved juices from the wok; mix well.

4 Pour the dressing over the seafood and toss gently. Arrange the salad leaves and cilantro sprigs on four individual plates, then spoon the seafood on top. Serve at once.

Whole-wheat Pasta, Asparagus, and Potato Salad with Parmesan

A meal in itself, this is a real treat when made with fresh asparagus just in season.

Serves 4

INGREDIENTS
½ lb whole-wheat pasta shapes
4 tbsp extra-virgin olive oil
salt and pepper
12 oz baby new potatoes
½ lb fresh asparagus
¼ lb piece fresh Parmesan cheese

olive oil

asparagus

Parmesan cheese

pasta shapes

new potatoes

1 Cook the pasta in boiling salted water according to the manufacturer's instructions. Drain well and toss with the olive oil, salt, and pepper while still warm.

2 Wash the potatoes and cook in boiling salted water for 12–15 minutes or until tender. Drain and toss with the pasta.

3 Trim any woody ends off the asparagus and halve the stalks if very long. Blanch in boiling salted water for 6 minutes until bright green and still crunchy. Drain. Plunge into cold water to stop them cooking and allow to cool. Drain and dry on paper towels.

4 Toss the asparagus with the potatoes and pasta, season, and transfer to a shallow bowl. Using a rotary vegetable peeler, shave the Parmesan cheese over the salad.

Mediterranean Salad with Basil

A type of Salade Niçoise with pasta, conjuring up all the sunny flavors of the Mediterranean.

Serves 4

INGREDIENTS
½ lb chunky pasta shapes
6 oz fine green beans
2 large ripe tomatoes
2 oz fresh basil leaves
7 oz can tuna fish in oil, drained
2 hard-cooked eggs, shelled and sliced
    or quartered
2 oz can anchovies, drained
capers and black olives

DRESSING
6 tbsp extra-virgin olive oil
2 tbsp white-wine vinegar or lemon
    juice
2 garlic cloves, crushed
½ tsp Dijon mustard
2 tbsp chopped fresh basil
salt and pepper

tomatoes

olive oil

garlic

basil

pasta

egg

anchovies

green beans

tuna fish

1 Whisk all the ingredients for the dressing together and leave to infuse while you make the salad.

2 Cook the pasta in plenty of boiling salted water according to the manufacturer's instructions. Drain well and cool.

3 Trim the beans and blanch in boiling salted water for 3 minutes. Drain and refresh in cold water.

4 Slice or quarter the tomatoes and arrange on the bottom of a bowl. Toss with a little dressing and cover with a quarter of the basil leaves. Then cover with the beans. Toss with a little more dressing and cover with a third of the remaining basil.

5 Cover with the pasta tossed in a little more dressing, half the remaining basil and the roughly flaked tuna.

6 Arrange the eggs on top, then finally scatter over the anchovies, capers and black olives. Pour over the remaining dressing and garnish with the remaining basil. Serve immediately. Don't be tempted to chill this salad – all the flavor will be dulled.

Broiled Bell Pepper Salad

Broiled bell peppers are delicious served hot with a sharp dressing. You can also eat them cold.

Serves 2

INGREDIENTS
1 red bell pepper
1 green bell pepper
1 yellow or orange bell pepper
½ radicchio, separated into leaves
½ frisée, separated into leaves
1½ tsp white wine vinegar
2 tbsp extra virgin olive oil
6 oz goat cheese
salt and freshly ground black pepper

frisée

green bell pepper

red bell pepper

yellow bell pepper

goat cheese

radicchio

white wine vinegar

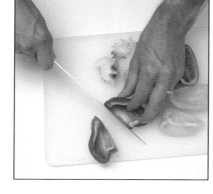

1 Preheat the broiler. Cut all the bell peppers in half. Cut each half into pieces.

2 Put the pepper pieces on a rack set over a broiler pan. Broil for 10 minutes.

3 Meanwhile, divide the radicchio and frisée leaves between two plates. Chill until required.

4 Mix the vinegar and olive oil in a jar. Add salt and pepper to taste. Close the jar tightly, and shake well.

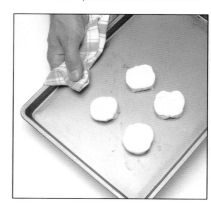

5 Slice the goat cheese, and place on a baking sheet. Broil for 1 minute.

6 Arrange the peppers and broiled goat cheese on the salads. Pour over the dressing, and grind a little extra black pepper over each.

COOK'S TIP
Broil the bell peppers until they just start to blacken around the edges – don't let them burn.

Parmesan and Poached Egg Salad with Croûtons

Soft poached eggs, hot garlic croûtons and cool, crisp salad leaves make an unforgettable combination.

Serves 2

INGREDIENTS
½ small loaf white bread
5 tbsp extra virgin olive oil
2 eggs
4 oz mixed salad leaves
2 garlic cloves, crushed
½ tbsp white wine vinegar
1 oz Parmesan cheese

Parmesan cheese

mixed salad leaves

white bread

garlic cloves

eggs

1 Remove the crust from the bread. Cut the bread into 1 in cubes.

2 Heat 2 tbsp of the oil in a frying pan. Cook the bread for about 5 minutes, tossing the cubes occasionally, until they are golden brown.

3 Meanwhile, bring a pan of water to a boil. Carefully slide in the eggs, one at a time. Gently poach the eggs for 4 minutes until lightly cooked.

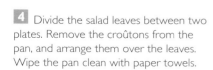

4 Divide the salad leaves between two plates. Remove the croûtons from the pan, and arrange them over the leaves. Wipe the pan clean with paper towels.

5 Heat the remaining oil in the pan, add the garlic and vinegar, and cook over high heat for 1 minute. Pour the warm dressing over each salad.

COOK'S TIP
Add a dash of vinegar to the water before poaching the eggs. This helps to keep the whites together. To make sure that a poached egg has a good shape, swirl the water with a spoon, whirlpool-fashion, before sliding in the egg.

6 Place a poached egg on each salad. Sprinkle with shavings of Parmesan and freshly ground black pepper, if desired.

Penne with Spinach

Serves 4

INGREDIENTS
8 ounces fresh spinach
1 garlic clove, crushed
1 shallot or small onion,
    finely chopped
$1/2$ small red bell pepper, seeded and
    finely chopped
1 small red chili, seeded
    and chopped
$2/3$ cup stock
12 ounces penne
5 ounces smoked turkey bacon
3 tablespoons low-fat sour cream
2 tablespoons grated
    Parmesan cheese
shavings of Parmesan cheese,
    to garnish

2 Put the garlic, shallot or small onion, pepper and chili into a large frying pan. Add the stock, cover and cook for about 5 minutes until tender. Add the prepared spinach and cook quickly for another 2–3 minutes until it has wilted.

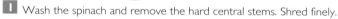

1 Wash the spinach and remove the hard central stems. Shred finely.

red bell pepper

grated Parmesan cheese

red chilies

shallot

smoked turkey bacon

penne

stock

low-fat sour cream

garlic

spinach

3 Cook the pasta in a large pan of boiling, salted water until *al dente*. Drain thoroughly.

4 Fry the smoked turkey bacon, cool a little, and chop finely.

5 Stir the sour cream and grated Parmesan into the pasta with the spinach, and toss carefully together.

6 Transfer to serving plates and sprinkle with chopped turkey and shavings of Parmesan cheese.

Green Pasta with Avocado Sauce

This is an unusual sauce with a pale green color, studded with red tomato. It has a luxurious velvety texture. The sauce is rich, so you don't need much for a filling meal.

Serves 6

INGREDIENTS
3 ripe tomatoes
2 large ripe avocados
2 tbsp butter, plus extra for tossing
   the pasta
1 garlic clove, crushed
1½ cups heavy cream
salt and pepper
dash of Tabasco sauce
1 lb green tagliatelle
freshly grated Parmesan cheese
4 tbsp sour cream

tagliatelle

tomatoes

avocado

garlic

1 Halve the tomatoes and remove the cores. Squeeze out the seeds and cut the tomatoes into dice. Set aside.

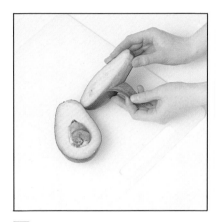

2 Halve the avocados, take out the pits, and peel. Roughly chop the flesh.

3 Melt the butter in a saucepan and add the garlic. Cook for 1 minute, then add the cream and chopped avocados. Raise the heat, stirring constantly to break up the avocados.

4 Add the diced tomatoes and season to taste with salt, pepper, and a little Tabasco sauce. Keep warm.

5 Cook the pasta in plenty of boiling salted water according to the manufacturer's instructions. Drain well and toss with a knob of butter.

6 Divide the pasta between 4 warmed bowls and spoon over the sauce. Sprinkle with grated Parmesan and top with a spoonful of sour cream.

Pasta with Shrimp and Feta Cheese

This dish combines the richness of fresh shrimp with the tartness of feta cheese. Goat cheese could be used as an alternative.

Serves 4

INGREDIENTS
1 lb medium raw shrimp
6 scallions
4 tbsp butter
½ lb feta cheese
salt and pepper
small bunch fresh chives
1 lb penne, garganelle, or rigatoni

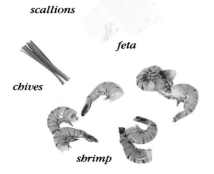

penne

scallions

feta

chives

shrimp

1 Remove the heads from the shrimp by twisting and pulling off. Peel the shrimp and discard the shells. Chop the scallions.

2 Melt the butter in a skillet and stir in the shrimp. When they turn pink, add the scallions and cook gently for 1 minute.

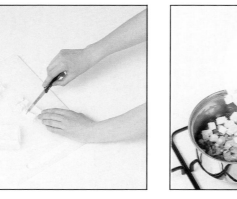

3 Cut the feta into ½ in cubes.

4 Stir the feta cheese into the shrimp mixture, and season with plenty of black pepper.

5 Cut the chives into 1 in lengths and stir half into the shrimp.

6 Cook the pasta in plenty of boiling salted water according to the manufacturer's instructions. Drain well, pile into a warmed serving dish, and top with the sauce. Scatter with the remaining chives and serve.

Mushroom Bolognese

A quick – and exceedingly tasty – vegetarian
version of the classic Italian meat dish.

Serves 4

INGREDIENTS
1 lb mushrooms
1 tbsp olive oil
1 onion, chopped
1 garlic clove, crushed
1 tbsp tomato paste
14 oz can chopped tomatoes
3 tbsp chopped fresh oregano
1 lb fresh pasta
Parmesan cheese, to serve
salt and freshly ground black pepper

mushrooms

chopped tomatoes

oregano

garlic clove

pasta

onion

Parmesan cheese

tomato paste

1 Trim the mushroom stems neatly.
Then cut each mushroom into quarters.

2 Heat the oil in a large pan. Add the
chopped onion and garlic, and cook for
2–3 minutes.

3 Add the mushrooms to the pan, and
cook over a high heat for 3–4 minutes,
stirring occasionally.

4 Stir in the tomato paste, chopped
tomatoes and 1 tbsp of the oregano.
Lower the heat, cover, and cook for
about 5 minutes.

5 Meanwhile, bring a large pan of
salted water to a boil. Cook the pasta for
2–3 minutes until just tender.

COOK'S TIP

If you prefer to use dried pasta, make this the first thing that you cook. It will take 10–12 minutes, during which time you can make the mushroom mixture. Use 12 oz dried pasta.

6 Season the bolognese sauce with salt and pepper. Drain the pasta, turn it into a bowl, and add the mushroom mixture. Toss to mix well. Serve in individual bowls, topped with shavings of fresh Parmesan and the remaining chopped fresh oregano.

Fettuccine all'Alfredo

A classic dish from Rome, Fettuccine all'Alfredo is simply pasta tossed with heavy cream, butter, and freshly grated Parmesan cheese. Popular less classic additions are peas and strips of ham.

Serves 4

INGREDIENTS
2 tbsp butter
⅔ cup heavy cream, plus 4 tbsp extra
1 lb fettuccine
freshly grated nutmeg
½ cup freshly grated Parmesan
  cheese, plus extra to serve
salt and pepper

fettuccine

nutmeg

Parmesan cheese

1 Place the butter and ⅔ cup cream in a heavy saucepan, bring to a boil, and simmer for 1 minute until slightly thickened.

2 Cook the fettuccine in plenty of boiling salted water according to the manufacturer's instructions, but for 2 minutes less time. The pasta should still be a little firm.

3 Drain very well and transfer to the pan with the cream sauce.

4 Place on the heat and toss the pasta in the sauce to coat.

5 Add the extra 4 tbsp cream, the cheese, salt and pepper to taste, and a little grated nutmeg. Toss until well coated and heated through. Serve immediately with extra grated Parmesan cheese.

Spaghetti Olio e Aglio

This is another classic recipe from Rome. A quick and filling dish, originally the food of the poor involving nothing more than pasta, garlic, and olive oil, but now fast becoming fashionable.

Serves 4

INGREDIENTS
2 garlic cloves
2 tbsp fresh parsley
½ cup olive oil
1 lb spaghetti
salt and pepper

spaghetti

olive oil

parsley

garlic

1 Finely chop the garlic.

2 Chop the parsley roughly.

3 Heat the olive oil in a medium saucepan and add the garlic and a pinch of salt. Cook gently, stirring all the time, until golden. If the garlic becomes too brown, it will taste bitter.

4 Meanwhile cook the spaghetti in plenty of boiling salted water according to the manufacturer's instructions. Drain well.

5 Toss with the warm – not sizzling – garlic and oil and add plenty of black pepper and the parsley. Serve immediately.

Double Tomato Tagliatelle

Sun-dried tomatoes add pungency to this dish, while the broiled fresh tomatoes add bite.

Serves 4

INGREDIENTS
3 tbsp olive oil
1 garlic clove, crushed
1 small onion, chopped
¼ cup dry white wine
6 sun-dried tomatoes, chopped
2 tbsp chopped fresh parsley
½ cup pitted black olives, halved
1 lb fresh tagliatelle
4 tomatoes, halved
Parmesan cheese, to serve
salt and freshly ground black pepper

tomatoes

parsley

garlic clove

sun-dried tomatoes

tagliatelle

dry white wine

onion

black olives

Parmesan cheese

COOK'S TIP

It is essential to buy Parmesan in a piece for this dish. Find a good source – fresh Parmesan should not be unacceptably hard – and shave or grate it yourself. The flavor will be much more intense than that of the pre-grated product.

1 Heat 2 tbsp of the oil in a pan. Add the garlic and onion, and cook for 2–3 minutes, stirring occasionally. Add the wine, sun-dried tomatoes and the parsley. Cook for 2 minutes. Stir in the black olives.

2 Bring a large pan of salted water to a boil. Add the fresh tagliatelle, and cook for 2–3 minutes until just tender. Preheat the broiler.

3 Put the tomatoes on a baking sheet, and brush with the remaining oil. Broil for 3–4 minutes.

4 Drain the pasta, return it to the pan, and toss with the sauce. Serve with the broiled tomatoes, freshly ground black pepper and shavings of Parmesan.

Spaghetti with Black Olive and Mushroom Sauce

A rich pungent sauce topped with sweet cherry tomatoes.

Serves 4

INGREDIENTS
1 tbsp olive oil
1 garlic clove, chopped
8 oz mushrooms, chopped
 generous ¹/₂ cup black olives, pitted
2 tbsp chopped fresh parsley
1 fresh red chili, seeded and chopped
1lb spaghetti
8 oz cherry tomatoes
slivers of Parmesan cheese, to serve
  (optional)

garlic

mushrooms

red chillies

cherry tomatoes

black olives

spaghetti

parsley

1 Heat the oil in a large pan. Add the garlic and cook for 1 minute. Add the mushrooms, cover, and cook over a medium heat for 5 minutes.

2 Place the mushrooms in a blender or food processor with the olives, parsley and red chili. Blend until smooth.

3 Cook the pasta following the instructions on the side of the package until *al dente*. Drain well and return to the pan. Add the olive mixture and toss together until the pasta is well coated. Cover and keep warm.

4 Heat an ungreased frying pan and shake the cherry tomatoes around until they start to split (about 2–3 minutes). Serve the pasta topped with the tomatoes and garnished with slivers of Parmesan, if desired.

Spinach and Ricotta Shells with Pine Nuts

Large pasta shells are designed to hold a variety of delicious stuffings. Few are more pleasing than this mixture of chopped spinach and ricotta cheese.

Serves 4

INGREDIENTS
12 oz large pasta shells
scant 2 cups crushed tomatoes or
    tomato purée
10 oz frozen chopped spinach,
    defrosted
2 oz crustless white bread, crumbled
½ cup milk
3 tbsp olive oil
2¼ cups ricotta cheese
pinch of nutmeg
1 garlic clove, crushed
1 tbsp olive oil
½ tsp black olive paste (optional)
¼ cup freshly grated Parmesan
    cheese
2 tbsp pine nuts
salt and freshly ground black pepper

olive paste

ricotta cheese

pine nuts

garlic

spinach

pasta shells

1 Bring a large saucepan of salted water to a boil. Toss in the pasta and cook according to the directions on the package. Refresh under cold water, drain and reserve until needed.

2 Pour the crushed tomatoes or purée into a nylon sieve over a bowl and strain to thicken. Place the spinach in another sieve and press out any excess liquid with the back of a spoon.

3 Place the bread, milk and oil in a food processor and combine. Add the spinach and ricotta and season with salt, pepper and nutmeg.

4 Combine the crushed tomatoes with the garlic, olive oil and olive paste if using. Spread the sauce evenly over the bottom of an ovenproof dish.

5 Spoon the spinach mixture into a piping bag fitted with a large plain nozzle and fill the pasta shapes (alternatively fill with a spoon). Arrange the pasta shapes over the sauce.

6 Preheat a moderate broiler. Heat the pasta through in a microwave oven at high power (100%) for 4 minutes. Scatter with Parmesan cheese and pine nuts, and finish under the broiler to brown the cheese.

Pasta with Pesto Sauce

Don't skimp on the fresh basil – this is the most wonderful sauce in the world! This pesto can also be used as a basting sauce for broiled chicken or fish, or rubbed over a leg of lamb before baking.

Serves 4

INGREDIENTS
2 garlic cloves
salt and pepper
½ cup pine nuts
1 cup fresh basil leaves
⅔ cup olive oil (not extra-virgin as it is too strong)
4 tbsp unsalted butter, softened
4 tbsp freshly grated Parmesan cheese
1 lb spaghetti

olive oil

spaghetti

pine nuts

Parmesan cheese

basil

1 Peel the garlic and process in a food processor with a little salt and the pine nuts until broken up. Add the basil leaves and continue mixing to a paste.

2 Gradually add the olive oil, little by little, until the mixture is creamy and thick.

3 Mix in the butter and season with pepper. Mix in the cheese. (Alternatively, you can make the pesto by hand using a pestle and mortar.)

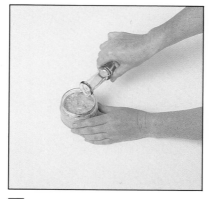

4 Store the pesto in a jar (with a layer of olive oil on top to exclude the air) in the fridge until needed.

5 Cook the pasta in plenty of boiling salted water according to the manufacturer's instructions. Drain well.

COOK'S TIP

A good pesto can be made using parsley instead of basil and walnuts instead of pine nuts. To make it go further, add a spoonful or two of fromage frais. 'Red' pesto includes sun-dried tomato paste and pounded roasted red peppers.

6 Toss the pasta with half the pesto and serve in warm bowls with the remaining pesto spooned on top.

Pasta Shells with Tomatoes and Arugula

This pretty-colored pasta dish relies for its success on a salad green called arugula. Available in large supermarkets, it is a leaf easily grown in the garden or a window box and tastes slightly peppery.

Serves 4

INGREDIENTS
1 lb shell pasta
salt and pepper
1 lb very ripe cherry tomatoes
3 tbsp olive oil
3 oz fresh arugula
Parmesan cheese

olive oil

pasta shells

cherry tomatoes

arugula

Parmesan cheese

1 Cook the pasta in plenty of boiling salted water according to the manufacturer's instructions. Drain well.

2 Halve the tomatoes. Trim, wash, and dry the arugula.

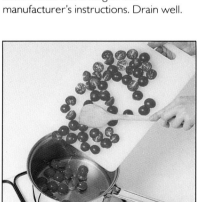

3 Heat the oil in a large saucepan, add the tomatoes, and cook for barely 1 minute. The tomatoes should only just heat through and not disintegrate.

4 Shave the Parmesan cheese using a rotary vegetable peeler.

5 Add the pasta, then the arugula. Carefully stir to mix and heat through. Season well with salt and freshly ground black pepper. Serve immediately with plenty of shaved Parmesan cheese.

Oriental Vegetable Noodles

Thin Italian egg pasta is a good alternative to Oriental egg noodles; use it fresh or dried.

Serves 6

INGREDIENTS
1 ¼ lb thin tagliarini
1 red onion
4 oz shiitake mushrooms
3 tbsp sesame oil
3 tbsp dark soy sauce
1 tbsp balsamic vinegar
2 tsp superfine sugar
1 tsp salt
celery leaves, to garnish

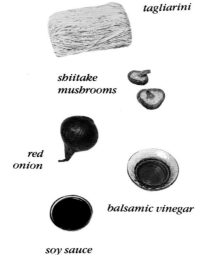

tagliarini

shiitake mushrooms

red onion

balsamic vinegar

soy sauce

1 Boil the tagliarini in a large pan of salted boiling water, following the instructions on the pack.

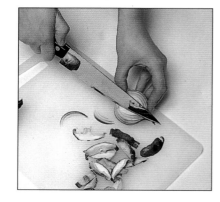

2 Thinly slice the red onion and the mushrooms, using a sharp knife.

3 Heat the wok, then add 1 tbsp of the sesame oil. When the oil is hot, stir-fry the onion and mushrooms for 2 minutes.

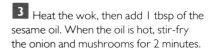

4 Drain the tagliarini, then add to the wok with the soy sauce, balsamic vinegar, sugar and salt. Stir-fry for 1 minute, then add the remaining sesame oil, and serve garnished with celery leaves.

Singapore Noodles

A delicious supper dish with a stunning mix of flavors and textures.

Serves 4

INGREDIENTS
8 oz dried egg noodles
3 tbsp peanut oil
1 onion, chopped
1-in piece fresh ginger,
    finely chopped
1 garlic clove,
    finely chopped
1 tbsp Madras curry powder
½ tsp salt
4 oz cooked chicken or pork,
    finely shredded
4 oz cooked peeled shrimp
4 oz Chinese cabbage leaves,
    shredded
4 oz beansprouts
4 tbsp chicken stock
1–2 tbsp dark soy sauce
1–2 fresh red chilies, seeded
    and finely shredded
4 scallions, finely shredded

beansprouts

Chinese cabbage

noodles

ginger

curry powder

chicken

dark soy sauce

onion

stock

scallions

red chilies

peanut oil

shrimp

1 Cook the noodles according to the package instructions. Rinse thoroughly under cold water and drain well. Toss in 1 tbsp of the oil and set aside.

2 Heat a wok until hot, add the remaining oil and swirl it around. Add the onion, ginger and garlic and stir-fry for about 2 minutes.

3 Add the curry powder and salt, stir-fry for 30 seconds, then add the egg noodles, chicken or pork and shrimp. Stir-fry for 3–4 minutes.

4 Add the Chinese cabbage and beansprouts and stir-fry for 1–2 minutes. Sprinkle in the stock and soy sauce to taste and toss well until evenly mixed. Serve at once, garnished with the shredded red chilies and scallions.

Kedgeree with Green Beans and Mushrooms

Crunchy green beans and mushrooms are the star ingredients in this vegetarian version of an old favorite.

Serves 2

INGREDIENTS
³/₄ cup basmati rice
1¹/₄ cups cold water
3 eggs
6 oz green beans, trimmed
¹/₄ cup butter
1 onion, finely chopped
8 oz crimini mushrooms, quartered
2 tbsp light cream
1 tbsp chopped fresh parsley
salt and freshly ground black pepper

light cream   crimini mushrooms   parsley

onion

butter

green beans

eggs

basmati rice

1 Wash the rice several times under cold running water. Drain thoroughly. Bring a pan of water to a boil. Add the rice, and cook for 10–12 minutes until tender. Drain thoroughly.

2 Half fill a second pan with water. Add the eggs, and bring to a boil. Lower the heat, and simmer for 8 minutes. Drain the eggs, and cool them under cold water. Remove the shells.

3 Bring another pan of water to a boil, and cook the green beans for 5 minutes. Drain, and refresh under cold running water. Then drain again.

4 Melt the butter in a large frying pan. Add the onions and mushrooms. Cook for 2–3 minutes over a moderate heat.

5 Add the green beans and rice to the onion mixture. Stir lightly to mix. Cook for 2 minutes. Cut the hard-boiled eggs in wedges, and add them to the pan.

6 Stir in the cream and parsley, taking care not to break up the eggs. Reheat the kedgeree, but do not allow it to boil. Serve at once.

Mixed Rice Noodles

A delicious noodle dish made extra special by adding avocado and garnishing with shrimp.

Serves 4

INGREDIENTS
1 tbsp sunflower oil
1 in piece ginger root, peeled
   and grated
2 cloves garlic, crushed
3 tbsp dark soy sauce
8 oz peas, thawed if frozen
1 lb rice noodles
1 lb fresh spinach, well washed and
   coarse stalks removed
2 tbsp smooth peanut butter
2 tbsp tahini
⅔ cup milk
1 ripe avocado, peeled and pitted
roasted peanuts and peeled shrimp,
   to garnish

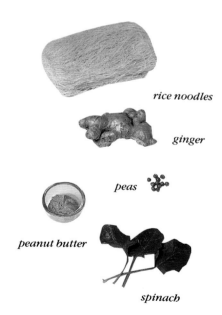

rice noodles

ginger

peas

peanut butter

spinach

1 Heat the wok, then add the oil. When the oil is fairly hot, stir-fry the ginger and garlic for approximately 30 seconds. Add 1 tbsp of the dark soy sauce and ⅔ cup boiling water.

2 Add the peas and noodles, then cook for 3 minutes. Stir in the spinach. Remove the vegetables and noodles, drain and keep warm.

3 Stir the peanut butter, remaining soy sauce, tahini and milk together in the wok, and simmer for 1 minute.

4 Add the vegetables and noodles, slice in the avocado and toss together. Serve piled on individual plates. Spoon some sauce over each portion and garnish with peanuts and shrimp.

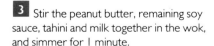

Capellini with Arugula, Snow Peas and Pine Nuts

A light but filling pasta dish with the added pepperiness of fresh arugula.

Serves 4

INGREDIENTS
9 oz capellini or angel-hair pasta
8 oz snow peas
6 oz arugula
¼ cup pine nuts, roasted
2 tbsp Parmesan cheese, finely grated (optional)
2 tbsp olive oil (optional)

arugula

Parmesan

pine nuts

capellini

snow peas

1 Cook the capellini or angel-hair pasta following the instructions on the side of the package until *al dente*.

2 Meanwhile, carefully top and tail the snow peas.

3 As soon as the pasta is cooked, drop in the arugula and snow peas. Drain immediately.

4 Toss the pasta with the roasted pine nuts, and Parmesan and olive oil if using. Serve at once.

COOK'S TIP
Olive oil and Parmesan are optional as they obviously raise the fat content.

Thai Fried Rice

This hot and spicy dish is easy to prepare and makes a meal in itself.

VARIATION
Add 2 oz frozen peas to the chicken in step 3, if you wish.

Serves 4

INGREDIENTS
8 oz Thai jasmine rice
3 tbsp vegetable oil
1 onion, chopped
1 small red bell pepper, seeded
 and cut into ¾-in cubes
12 oz skinless and boneless
 chicken breasts, cut into
 ¾-in cubes
1 garlic clove, crushed
1 tbsp mild curry paste
½ tsp paprika
½ tsp ground turmeric
2 tbsp Thai fish sauce
 (*nam pla*)
2 eggs, beaten
salt and ground black pepper
fried basil leaves, to garnish

rice

Thai fish sauce

chicken

curry paste

onion

egg

red pepper

turmeric

paprika

vegetable oil

1 Put the rice in a sieve and wash thoroughly under cold running water. Then put the rice in a heavy-bottomed pan and add 6¼ cups boiling water. Return to a boil, then simmer, leaving the pan uncovered, for 8–10 minutes; drain well. Spread out the grains on a tray and set aside to cool.

2 Heat a wok until hot, add 2 tbsp of the oil and swirl it around. Add the onion and red pepper and stir-fry for 1 minute.

3 Add the chicken, garlic, curry paste and spices and stir-fry for 2–3 minutes.

4 Reduce the heat to medium, add the cooled rice, fish sauce and seasoning. Stir-fry for 2–3 minutes, until the rice is very hot.

5 Make a well in the center of the rice and add the remaining oil. When hot, add the beaten eggs, allow to cook for about 2 minutes until lightly set, then stir into the rice.

6 Sprinkle over the fried basil leaves and serve at once.

Caramelized Apples

A sweet, sticky dessert which is very quickly made, and usually very quickly eaten!

Serves 4

INGREDIENTS
1½ lb sweet apples
½ cup unsalted butter
1 oz fresh white bread crumbs
½ cup ground almonds
rind of 2 lemons, finely grated
4 tbsp corn syrup
4 tbsp thick strained yogurt,
    to serve

lemon

corn syrup

ground almonds

apple

1 Peel and core the apples.

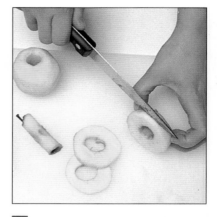

2 Carefully cut the apples into ½ in-thick rings.

3 Heat the wok, then add the butter. When the butter has melted, add the apple rings and stir-fry for 4 minutes until golden and tender. Remove from the wok, reserving the butter. Add the bread crumbs to the hot butter and stir-fry for 1 minute.

4 Stir in the ground almonds and lemon rind and stir-fry for a further 3 minutes, stirring constantly. Sprinkle the breadcrumb mix over the apples, then drizzle warmed corn syrup over the top. Serve with thick strained yogurt.

Fruit Kebabs with Chocolate and Marshmallow Fondue

Children love these treats – and with supervision they can help to make them.

Serves 4

2 bananas
2 kiwis
12 strawberries
1 tbsp melted butter
1 tbsp lemon juice
1 tsp ground cinnamon

FOR THE FONDUE
8 oz baking chocolate
½ cup light cream
8 marshmallows
½ tsp vanilla extract

baking chocolate

vanilla extract

bananas

lemon juice

ground cinnamon

melted butter

light cream

marshmallows

kiwis

strawberries

1 Peel the bananas and cut each into six thick chunks. Peel the kiwis thinly and quarter them. Thread the bananas, kiwis and strawberries onto four wooden or bamboo skewers.

2 Mix together the butter, lemon juice and cinnamon and brush the mixture over the fruits.

3 For the fondue, place the chocolate, cream and marshmallows in a small pan and heat gently on the barbecue, without boiling, stirring until the mixture has melted and is smooth.

4 Cook the kebabs on the barbecue for 2–3 minutes, turning once, or until golden. Stir the vanilla extract into the fondue and serve it with the kebabs.

Quick Apricot Blender Whip

One of the quickest desserts you could make – and also one of the prettiest.

Serves 4

INGREDIENTS
14 oz can apricot halves in juice
1 tbsp Grand Marnier or brandy
¾ cup plain strained yogurt
2 tbsp slivered almonds

yogurt

Grand Marnier

apricot halves

slivered almonds

I Drain the juice from the apricots and place the fruit and liqueur in a blender or food processor.

2 Process the apricots until smooth.

3 Spoon the fruit purée and yogurt in alternate spoonfuls into four tall glasses or glass dishes, swirling them together slightly to give a marbled effect.

4 Lightly toast the almonds until they are golden. Let them cool slightly and then sprinkle them on top.

COOK'S TIP

For an even lighter dessert, use low-fat instead of plain yogurt, and, if you prefer to omit the liqueur, add a little of the fruit juice from the can.

Chocolate Mousse on the Loose

Super-light, dark, creamy and delicious; the chocolate mousse is always popular and should maintain a high profile on any dessert menu.

Serves 4

INGREDIENTS

7 oz best quality plain chocolate, plus
    extra for flaking
3 eggs
2 tbsp dark rum or whisky
¼ cup superfine sugar
½ pint/1¼ cups whipping
    cream
confectioners' sugar, for dusting

plain chocolate

whipping cream

eggs

superfine sugar

1 Break the chocolate into a bowl, stand over a saucepan of simmering water and melt. Separate the egg whites into a large mixing bowl, remove the chocolate from the heat and stir in the egg yolks and alcohol.

2 Whisk the egg whites until firm, gradually add the sugar and whisk until stiff peaks form.

3 Whip the cream to a dropping consistency and set aside until required.

4 Give the egg whites a final beating with a rubber spatula, add the chocolate and fold all the ingredients together gently, retaining as much air as possible.

5 Fold in the loosely whipped cream, turn into four glasses or bowls and chill until ready to serve.

COOK'S TIP
It is a false economy to use inexpensive chocolate. Choose the best quality dark chocolate you can find and enjoy it!

6 Decorate with flaked chocolate and dust with confectioners' sugar.

Brazilian Coffee Bananas

Rich, lavish and sinful-looking, this dessert takes only about 2 minutes to make!

Serves 4

INGREDIENTS
4 small ripe bananas
1 tbsp instant coffee granules or
    powder
1 tbsp hot water
2 tbsp dark brown sugar
1⅛ cups strained plain yogurt
1 tbsp toasted slivered almonds

bananas

yogurt

slivered almonds

instant coffee

dark brown sugar

1 Peel and slice one banana and mash the remaining three with a fork.

2 Dissolve the coffee in the hot water and stir into the mashed bananas.

3 Spoon a little of the mashed banana mixture into four serving dishes and sprinkle with sugar. Top with a spoonful of yogurt, then repeat until all the ingredients are used up.

4 Swirl the last layer of yogurt for a marbled effect. Finish with a few banana slices and slivered almonds. Serve cold. Best eaten within about an hour of making.

VARIATION

For a special occasion, add a dash – just a dash – of dark rum or brandy to the bananas for extra richness.
1 tbsp of rum or brandy adds about 30 calories.

Barbecued Strawberry Croissants

A deliciously simple, sinful dessert.

Serves 4

4 croissants
1/2 cup ricotta cheese
1/2 cup strawberry preserves
   or jam

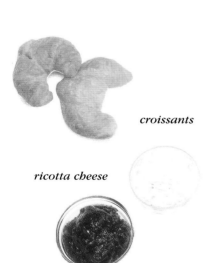

croissants

ricotta cheese

strawberry preserves

1 Split the croissants in half and open them out on a board.

2 Spread the bottom half of each croissant with ricotta cheese.

3 Top with a generous spoonful of strawberry preserves and replace the top half of the croissant.

4 Place the croissants on a hot barbecue and cook for 2–3 minutes, turning once.

COOK'S TIP

As an alternative to croissants, try fresh scones or muffins, toasted on the barbecue.

Mixed Melon Salad with Wild Strawberries

Ice-cold melon is a delicious way to end a meal. Here several varieties are combined with strongly flavored wild strawberries. If wild berries are not available, use ordinary strawberries or raspberries.

Serves 4

INGREDIENTS
1 cantaloupe or charentais melon
1 galia or Spanish melon
2 lb watermelon
6 oz wild strawberries
4 sprigs fresh mint

COOK'S TIP
Ripe melons should give slightly when pressed at the base, and should give off a fruity, melony scent. Buy carefully if you plan to use the fruit on the day.

wild strawberries

galia melon

mint

cantaloupe

watermelon

1 Halve the cantaloupe, galia, and watermelons.

2 Remove the seeds from the cantaloupe and galia with a spoon.

3 With a melon-baller, take out as many balls as you can from all 3 melons. Combine in a large bowl and refrigerate.

4 Add the wild strawberries and transfer to 4 stemmed glass dishes.

5 Decorate with sprigs of mint.

Pineapple Wedges with Rum Butter Glaze

Fresh pineapple is even more full of flavor when grilled; this spiced rum glaze makes it into a very special dessert.

Serves 4

1 medium pineapple
2 tbsp dark raw sugar
1 tsp ground ginger
4 tbsp melted butter
2 tbsp dark rum

pineapple

 With a large, sharp knife, cut the pineapple lengthwise into four wedges. Cut out and discard the center core.

melted butter

dark raw sugar

ground ginger   *dark rum*

 Cut between the flesh and skin, to release the flesh, but leave the skin in place. Slice the flesh across, into chunks.

COOK'S TIP

For an easier version, simply cut off the skin and then slice the whole pineapple into thick slices and cook as above.

 Push a bamboo skewer lengthwise through each wedge and into the stalk, to hold the chunks in place.

Mix together the sugar, ginger, melted butter and rum and brush over the pineapple. Cook the wedges on a hot barbecue for 3–4 minutes; pour the remaining glaze over the top and serve.

Nectarines with Marzipan and Mascarpone

A luscious dessert that no one can resist – dieters may like to use low-fat soft cheese or ricotta instead of mascarpone.

Serves 4

4 firm, ripe nectarines or
 peaches
3 oz marzipan
5 tbsp mascarpone cheese
3 macaroons crushed

mascarpone cheese

nectarines

marzipan

macaroons

1 Cut the nectarines or peaches in half, removing the pits.

2 Cut the marzipan into eight pieces and press one piece into the pit cavity of each nectarine half.

COOK'S TIP
Either peaches or nectarines can be used for this recipe. If the pit does not pull out easily when you halve the fruit, use a small, sharp knife to cut around it.

3 Spoon the mascarpone on top. Sprinkle the crushed macaroons over the mascarpone.

4 Place the half-fruits on a hot barbecue for 3–5 minutes, until they are hot and the mascarpone starts to melt.

Prune and Orange Whip

A simple, storecupboard dessert, made in minutes.
It can be served immediately, but it's best chilled
for about half an hour before serving.

Serves 4

INGREDIENTS
1 ½ cups ready-to-eat dried prunes
⅔ cup orange juice
1 cup low-fat plain yogurt
shreds of orange rind, to decorate

orange rind

plain yogurt

orange juice

prunes

1 Remove the pits from the prunes and roughly chop them. Place them in a pan with the orange juice.

2 Bring the juice to a boil, stirring. Reduce the heat, cover and leave to simmer for 5 minutes, until the prunes are tender and the liquid is reduced by half.

3 Remove from the heat, allow to cool slightly and then beat well with a wooden spoon, until the fruit breaks down to a rough purée.

VARIATION
This dessert can also be made with other ready-to-eat dried fruit, such as apricots or peaches. For a special occasion, add a dash of brandy or Cointreau with the yogurt.

4 Transfer the mixture to a bowl. Stir in the yogurt, swirling the yogurt and fruit purée together lightly, to give a marbled effect.

5 Spoon the mixture into stemmed glasses or individual dishes, smoothing the tops.

6 Top each pot with a few shreds of orange rind, to decorate. Chill before serving.

Mango and Coconut Stir-fry

Choose a ripe mango for this recipe. If you buy one
that is a little under-ripe, leave it in a warm place for
a day or two before using.

Serves 4

INGREDIENTS
¼ coconut
1 large, ripe mango
juice of 2 limes
rind of 2 limes, finely grated
1 tbsp sunflower oil
1 tbsp butter
1½ tbsp honey
sour cream or yogurt, to serve

coconut

mango

honey

lime

COOK'S TIP

Because of the delicate taste of
desserts, always make sure your wok
has been scrupulously cleaned so
there is no transference of flavors –
a garlicky mango isn't quite the effect
you want to achieve!

1 Prepare the coconut shreds by
draining the milk from the coconut and
shredding the flesh with a peeler.

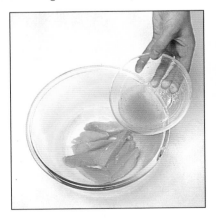

3 Place the mango slices in a bowl and
pour over the lime juice and rind, to
marinate them.

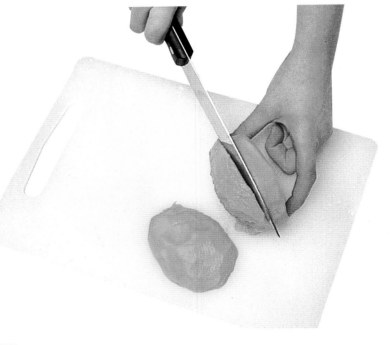

2 Peel the mango. Cut the pit out of the middle of the fruit.
Cut each half of the mango into slices.

4 Meanwhile, heat the wok, then add
2 tsp of the oil. When the oil is hot, add
the butter. When the butter has melted,
stir in the coconut shreds and stir-fry for
1–2 minutes until the coconut is golden
brown. Remove and drain on paper
towels. Wipe out the wok. Strain the
mango slices, reserving the juice.

5 Heat the wok and add the remaining
oil. When the oil is hot, add the mango
and stir-fry for 1–2 minutes, then add the
juice and allow to bubble and reduce for
1 minute. Then stir in the honey, sprinkle
on the coconut and serve with sour
cream or yogurt.

Apples and Raspberries in Rose Pouchong Syrup

Inspiration for this dessert stems from the fact that the apple and the raspberry belong to the rose family. The subtle flavors are shared here in an infusion of rose-scented tea.

Serves 4

INGREDIENTS
1 tsp rose pouchong tea
1 tsp rose water (optional)
¼ cup sugar
1 tsp lemon juice
5 dessert apples
1½ cups fresh raspberries

tea

apples

sugar

raspberries

COOK'S TIP
If fresh raspberries are out of season, use the same weight of frozen fruit or a 14 oz can of well drained fruit.

1 Warm a large tea pot. Add the rose pouchong tea and 3¾ cups of boiling water together with the rose water, if using. Allow the tea to stand and infuse for 4 minutes.

2 Measure the sugar and lemon juice into a stainless steel saucepan. Strain in the tea and stir to dissolve the sugar.

3 Peel and core the apples, then cut into quarters.

4 Poach the apples in the syrup for about 5 minutes.

5 Transfer the apples and syrup to a large metal tray and leave to cool to room temperature.

6 Pour the cooled apples and syrup into a bowl, add the raspberries and mix to combine. Spoon into individual glass dishes or bowls and serve warm.

Cherry Crêpes

These crêpes are virtually fat-free, and lower in calories and higher in fiber than traditional ones. Serve with plain yogurt or fromage frais.

Serves 4

INGREDIENTS
FOR THE CRÊPES
½ cup all-purpose flour
⅓ cup all-purpose whole wheat flour
pinch of salt
1 egg white
⅔ cup skim milk
⅔ cup water
a little oil for frying

FOR THE FILLING
15 oz can black cherries in juice
1½ tsp arrowroot

skim milk

whole wheat flour

all-purpose flour

black cherries

arrowroot

egg

1 Sift the flours and salt into a bowl, adding any bran left in the sifter to the bowl at the end.

2 Make a well in the center of the flour and add the egg white. Gradually beat in the milk and water, whisking hard until all the liquid is incorporated and the batter is smooth and bubbly.

3 Heat a non-stick pan with a small amount of oil until the pan is very hot. Pour in just enough batter to cover the base of the pan, swirling the pan to cover the base evenly.

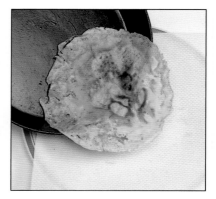

4 Cook until the crêpe is set and golden, and then turn to cook the other side. Remove to a sheet of paper towel and then cook the remaining batter to make about eight crêpes.

5 Drain the cherries, reserving the juice. Blend about 2 tbsp of the juice from the can of cherries with the arrowroot in a saucepan. Stir in the rest of the juice. Heat gently, stirring, until boiling. Stir over moderate heat for about 2 minutes, until thickened and clear.

COOK'S TIP

If fresh cherries are in season, cook them gently in enough apple juice just to cover them, and then thicken the juice with arrowroot as in Step 5.

The basic crêpes will freeze very successfully. Layer them with paper towels or wax paper, overwrap them in plastic wrap and seal. Freeze for up to six months. Thaw at room temperature.

6 Add the cherries and stir until thoroughly heated. Spoon the cherries into the crêpes and fold them in quarters.

INDEX